Southern Living.

The
SOUTHERN
HERITAGE
COOKBOOK
LIBRARY

The SOUTHERN HERITAGE
Cakes
COOKBOOK

OXMOOR HOUSE, INC.
Birmingham, Alabama

Southern Living ®

The Southern Heritage Cookbook Library

Copyright 1983 by Oxmoor House, Inc.
Book Division of Southern Progress Corporation
P.O. Box 2262, Birmingham, Alabama 35201

Southern Living ® is a federally registered trademark belonging to
Southern Living, Inc.

Library of Congress Catalog Number: 82-62141
ISBN: 0-8487-0601-3

Manufactured in the United States of America

The Southern Heritage CAKES Cookbook

Manager, Editorial Projects: Ann H. Harvey
Southern Living ® *Foods Editor:* Jean W. Liles
Editors: Katherine M. Eakin, Annette Thompson
Director, Test Kitchen: Laura N. Nestelroad
Test Kitchen Home Economists: Pattie B. Booker,
   Elizabeth J. Taliaferro, Kay E. Clarke
Production Manager: Jerry R. Higdon
Editorial Assistant: Melinda E. West
Food Photographer: Jim Bathie
Food Stylist: Sara Jane Ball
Layout Designer: Christian von Rosenvinge
Mechanical Artist: Faith Nance
Research Assistant: Janice Randall

Special Consultants

Art Director: Irwin Glusker
Heritage Consultant: Meryle Evans
Foods Writer: Lillian B. Marshall
Food and Recipe Consultants: Marilyn Wyrick Ingram, Audrey P. Stehle

Cover (clockwise from back): Miss Arintha's Birthday Cake (page 104),
General Robert E. Lee Cake (page 18), Hot Water Gingerbread (page 65), and
Martha Washington's Great Cake (page 90). Photograph by George Ratkai.

CONTENTS

INTRODUCTION

While the stately Mount Vernon Cake or the exotic Japanese Fruitcake may appear but rarely on the company menu these days, the art of cake baking remains a point of great pride among Southern hostesses. As the life-styles and roles of women have evolved, so have the tools and appliances with which they furnish their kitchens. Even the ingredients used in grandmother's recipes have changed. Flour is uniformly fine, soda has gained respectability, and somebody finally combined soda with cream of tartar to make baking powder that performs predictably and consistently.

What remains for the Southern cake baker is the bred-in-the-bone pride of accomplishment and, most importantly, the quality. Guesswork in baking lives in the past. Ovens with thermostats prepare a "quick" or "slow" oven on demand, and electric appliances make short work of the arm-numbing task of beating the ingredients. Finally, thanks to the pioneering work of Fannie Merritt Farmer, standard measuring spoons and cups have replaced grandmother's dessert spoon, wine glass, and goblet.

One doesn't have to be terribly gifted anymore, then, in order to serve up an impressive powder puff of an angel food cake or a buttery pound cake. All that is necessary is a little attention to detail. Baking is now, as the old phrase has it, "a job with the work picked out."

It can be said, and frequently is, that there are two basic kinds of cake: butter and sponge. Variations abound, but they are almost certainly traceable back to the basics.

Instead of butter and sponge, think of fat and lean. Imagine Jack Sprat's doctor saying, "Mr. Sprat, if you don't cut down on your cholesterol intake, I cannot take the responsibility for your health. No more egg yolks for you; no more butter." Angel food cake, which is purely American in origin, could have been the saving grace of Jack Sprat's diet, but alas, the Sprats were not only fictional, but also English. Consequently, they could have known neither cholesterol nor angel food cakes. Mrs. Sprat, under the same circumstances, was deprived of the glories of pound cake, with a whole pound of butter baked into it.

Old recipes for butter cakes instruct the cook to "rub the butter and sugar to a cream," or to cream the butter, "throwing in the sugar a little at a time, until the grains of sugar may no longer be felt." Does this inform us that the human hand was the only implement suitable for the creaming process? Not necessarily, although it was used with excellent results.

Marion Harland, writing in *Common Sense in the Household* in 1873, said "Stir the butter and sugar to a cream . . . use only a silver or wooden spoon in this as in other parts of your work." This admonition was followed by a prophecy: "I have heard of silver egg whips, but they are not likely to come into general use."

In Harland's opinion, " . . . all kinds of cake are better for having the whites and yolks beaten separately." Parenthetically, it is worth noting that by the mid-1800s, most American food writers had begun to call a yolk a "yolk," departing from the traditional English spelling, "yelk." The whites should be beaten "in a large shallow dish until you can cut through the froth with a knife, leaving as clear and distinct an incision as you would in a solid substance." Tennis elbow sufferers must have been legion among those who had never seen a tennis court, but that is merely conjecture.

Fifty-five years after *Common Sense in the Household* was published, Henrietta Stanley Dull contradicted Harland's advice on eggs in cake baking in her splendid book *Southern Cooking:* "Some of the recipes in this book call for the frothed egg whites, some not. Being the original recipes, they were left just as they were. I use these recipes without frothing or separating the eggs, with success." She went on to except sponge cakes from this, noting that "air is usually the only leavening in them."

Another of Dull's theories not in general use today is that all cakes should be started in an oven "just warm. . . a hot oven causes cake to bake at the edge and stick to pan and not rise at the sides. Consequently it will be compelled to rise up in the center. A cool oven allows the cake to rise with the heating of the oven and become level before oven is hot enough to bake."

Many "improved" models of egg beaters had been invented before, but the Dover rotary beater finally arrived in 1870. It was greeted by cooks with the kind of joyous abandon with which our generation has embraced the food processor. Dependable baking powder was only a decade or so away. The two together, labor saver and predictable leavening power, helped to bring Southern cake baking to its flowering.

Looking back, we may wonder why baking powder was so long in coming; it is only baking soda and cream of tartar with flour or starch added, all of which were in common use. One reason may be that the alkaline precursors of refined bicarbonate of soda, such as saleratus and pearl ash, were so despised by purists.

Reason was perhaps on the side of those purists: saleratus was a crude sodium of uncertain power that sometimes imparted an unpleasant flavor of its own. Pearl ash, a potassium carbonate made by partially purifying potash from wood ashes, was regarded by some as being too near a relative of lye. At best, both were looked down upon as easy ways out for the proper beating of eggs. But the one-piece leaven in a can labeled "baking powder" was still in the future.

Dr. Austen Church started marketing his "Arm & Hammer" baking soda in the early 1830s. The package carried the word "soda" on one side and "saleratus" on the other. A recipe booklet from Church & Co. dated 1884 contains dire warnings against baking powder, citing the large increase in its use during recent years, and calling its manufacturers to account for "grossly" adulterating the product. The adulterant was, of course, starch, and it still is; it keeps the powder dry!

By the time the nineteenth century became the twentieth, Southern cake bakers were armed with mechanical egg beaters and reliable baking powder. Some of the more affluent were presiding over imposing cast-iron stoves. At this point, if they had taken to heart the advice of Marion Harland to "study the moods and tenses of your oven carefully before essaying a loaf of cake," they were ready for the new wave of experimentation to follow.

The time was ripe for the development of tender layer cakes for which the South is famous. A list of these creations reads like a culinary jewelry catalogue: Dolly Varden, namesake of the heroine of Dickens' *Barnaby Rudge*; Lady and Lord Baltimore, that handsome and enduring pair that keeps us from wasting yolks or whites. Add La Reine Cake and White Mountain Cake and Lane Cake, those ephemeral but lasting monuments to Southern inventiveness. We have inherited a whole bookful of them, and the Southern hostess is aware that to produce one of these showpieces is to prove that she "keeps a good table."

GREAT LAYER CAKES

C all us shameless name droppers, but Southerners have a habit of honoring places and people, real or fictional, by naming cakes after them. Take the cake, Minnehaha. Longfellow's poem *Hiawatha* was published in 1855. For nigh a hundred years, schoolchildren, North and South, memorized and intoned it, immortalizing not only Hiawatha's beloved, but unknowingly, the waterfall in Minnesota for which the poet named her.

When Charles Dickens wrote *Barnaby Rudge* in 1841, Southerners took the heroine, Dolly Varden, to their hearts, and eventually baked her a cake. Dickens wrote *American Notes* in 1842 after a trip to this country, during which he visited Louisville where he was a guest at the Galt House.

But what of our Baltimore cakes? There's a poser. Charles Calvert, the third Lord Baltimore, was sent from England in 1661 to govern the territory granted his grandfather by King James, the land that was to become Maryland. By all accounts, his rule was so despotic that his subjects hated him, and he finally had to flee to England after a run-in with William Penn over the northern boundary of his land grant. Who would name cakes for such a Lord and his Lady? More than likely the cakes were called after the regal city their Lordships had named for themselves.

We have a cake for Williamsburg, the exquisite city where so many important events in our history took place. We have cakes for our heroes, of course: General Robert E. Lee and Sam Houston, that unique, high-principled soldier and statesman. And cakes for gallant women: Alabamian Emma Rylander Lane, and Jennie Benedict of Louisville, who destitute, parlayed her home baking into the most elegant tearoom and catering establishment in town.

Typically Southern is the inclusion of that combination we have loved so long, coconut and orange. Find it in the Ambrosia Cake and the romantic Moss Rose. Even Tutti Frutti is literally "all fruit" in Italian. Chocolate Yeast Cake dates back to pre-baking powder days when the baker held out a lump of bread dough to make a cake.

These heirloom recipes are legacies from great grandmothers whose sphere of influence did not reach far from home. They are significant in that a woman's baking and entertaining sometimes comprised her only creative outlet.

Front to back: Minnehaha Cake (page 19), Japanese Fruitcake (page 25), once called Oriental Cake, and Chocolate Yeast Cake (page 27), originally made with leftover yeast dough.

NAME DROPPING

LADY BALTIMORE CAKE

¾ cup shortening
2 cups sugar
3 cups sifted cake flour
1 tablespoon baking powder
½ teaspoon salt
½ cup milk
½ cup water
1 teaspoon vanilla extract
6 egg whites
Filling (recipe follows)
Frosting (recipe follows)
Walnut halves

Cream shortening; gradually add sugar, beating well.

Combine flour, baking powder, and salt. Combine milk and water. Add flour mixture to creamed mixture alternately with milk mixture, beginning and ending with flour mixture. Beat well after each addition. Stir in vanilla.

Beat egg whites (at room temperature) until stiff peaks form; fold into batter. Pour batter into 3 greased and floured 9-inch round cakepans. Bake at 350° for 25 minutes or until a wooden pick inserted in center comes out clean. Cool in pans 10 minutes; remove layers from pans, and let cool completely. Spread filling between layers; cover top and sides with frosting. Garnish with reserved filling and walnut halves. Yield: one 3-layer cake.

Filling:

1½ cups sugar
⅛ teaspoon cream of tartar
¼ cup plus 2 tablespoons water
2 egg whites
1 teaspoon vanilla extract
½ teaspoon lemon extract
1½ cups chopped pecans
1 cup chopped raisins
1 cup chopped figs

Combine sugar, cream of tartar, and water in a heavy saucepan. Cook over medium heat, stirring frequently, until mixture comes to a boil and the sugar is dissolved. Continue cooking, stirring frequently,

Lady Baltimore Cake pictured on the piazza of the Judge Robert Pringle home in Charleston, South Carolina.

until the mixture reaches soft ball stage (240°).

Beat egg whites (at room temperature) until foamy. While beating at medium speed of electric mixer, slowly pour hot syrup in a thin stream over egg whites. Turn mixer to high speed and continue beating until stiff peaks form. Add flavorings; beat until blended. Stir in remaining ingredients. Reserve ¼ cup prepared filling for garnish. Yield: enough for one 3-layer cake.

Frosting:

1 cup sugar
1 egg white
1 tablespoon light corn syrup
⅛ teaspoon salt
3 tablespoons cold water
1 teaspoon vanilla extract

Combine sugar, egg white (at room temperature), corn syrup, and salt in top of a large double boiler; add cold water, and beat on low speed of electric mixer for 30 seconds or just until blended.

Place over boiling water; beat on high speed of electric mixer about 7 minutes or until stiff peaks form. Remove from heat, and place over cold water; let stand about 5 minutes. Stir in vanilla. Spoon warm frosting on cooled cake. Yield: enough for one 3-layer cake.

LORD BALTIMORE CAKE

¾ cup butter, softened
1¼ cups sugar
8 egg yolks
2½ cups sifted cake flour
1 tablespoon baking
  powder
½ teaspoon salt
¾ cup milk
½ teaspoon lemon extract
Lord Baltimore Filling

Cream butter; gradually add sugar, beating well. Beat egg yolks until thick and lemon colored, and add to creamed mixture. Beat well.

Combine dry ingredients; add to creamed mixture alternately with milk, beginning and ending with flour mixture. Stir in lemon extract.

Pour batter into 3 greased and floured 9-inch round cakepans. Bake at 350° for 20 to 25 minutes or until a wooden pick inserted in center comes out clean. Cool in pans 10 minutes; remove layers from pans, and let cool completely. Spread Lord Baltimore Filling between layers and on top of cake. Yield: one 3-layer cake.

Lord Baltimore Filling:

1½ cups sugar
1 tablespoon light corn
  syrup
½ cup water
2 egg whites
¼ teaspoon orange juice
2 teaspoons lemon juice
12 candied cherries, chopped
½ cup macaroon crumbs
½ cup almonds, chopped and
  toasted
½ cup pecans, chopped

Combine sugar, syrup, and water in a small saucepan; cook over low heat until mixture reaches soft ball stage (240°).

Beat egg whites (at room temperature) until soft peaks form. While beating at medium speed of electric mixer, slowly pour hot syrup mixture in a thin stream over egg whites. Beat 1 minute. Combine remaining ingredients; fold into filling. Yield: enough for one 3-layer cake.

"**I** stepped forward to the counter, adventurous, but polite.

'I should like a slice, if you please, of Lady Baltimore,' I said with extreme formality.

"I thought she was going to burst; after a second she replied, 'Certainly,' . . . . "

". . . I returned to the table and she brought me the cake, and I had my first felicitous meeting with Lady Baltimore. Oh, my goodness! Did you ever taste it? It's all soft, and it's in layers, and it has nuts—but I can't write any more about it; my mouth waters too much. . . . "

Lady Baltimore, by Owen Wister, 1906

JENNIE BENEDICT'S RUM CAKE

1 cup butter or margarine,
  softened
2 cups sugar
3½ cups sifted cake flour
1 tablespoon baking powder
Pinch of salt
1 cup milk
1 teaspoon vanilla extract
8 egg whites
Filling (recipe follows)
Frosting (recipe follows)

Cream butter; gradually add sugar, beating well.

Combine flour, baking powder, and salt; add to creamed mixture alternately with milk, beginning and ending with flour mixture. Stir in vanilla.

Beat egg whites (at room temperature) until stiff peaks form; fold into batter.

Spoon batter into 2 waxed paper-lined and greased 9-inch round cakepans. Bake at 350° for 35 minutes or until a wooden pick inserted in center comes out clean. Cool in pans 10 minutes; remove from pans, and cool completely.

Spread filling between layers of cake, and chill. Spread top and sides of cake with frosting. Yield: one 2-layer cake.

Filling:

⅔ cup butter or margarine,
  softened
2½ cups sifted powdered
  sugar
¼ cup light rum

Combine all ingredients, beating until smooth. Chill. Yield: about 1½ cups.

Frosting:

2 cups sugar
2 egg whites
1 cup water
1½ teaspoons light rum

Combine sugar and egg whites (at room temperature) in top of a double boiler; add water, and beat on low speed of electric mixer for 30 seconds or just until blended.

Place over boiling water; beat constantly on high speed of electric mixer about 7 minutes or until stiff peaks form. Remove from heat. Add rum, and beat 2 additional minutes or until frosting is thick enough to spread. Yield: enough for one 2-layer cake.

LANE CAKE

1 cup butter or margarine, softened
2 cups sugar
3¼ cups sifted cake flour
2 teaspoons baking powder
Pinch of salt
1 cup milk
2 teaspoons vanilla extract
8 egg whites (reserve yolks for filling)
Filling (recipe follows)
Frosting (recipe follows)

Cream butter; gradually add sugar, beating with electric mixer until light and fluffy.

Combine dry ingredients. Add flour mixture to creamed mixture alternately with milk, beginning and ending with flour mixture. Stir in vanilla.

Beat egg whites (at room temperature) until stiff peaks form; fold into batter.

Pour batter into 3 greased and floured 9-inch round cakepans. Bake at 375° for 20 minutes or until a wooden pick inserted in center comes out clean. Cool in pans 10 minutes; remove from pans, and let cool completely.

Spread filling between layers of cake; spread top and sides of cake with frosting. Yield: one 3-layer cake.

Filling:

8 egg yolks
1 cup sugar
½ cup butter or margarine
1 cup maraschino cherries, finely chopped
1 cup finely chopped pecans
¾ cup raisins, finely chopped
¾ cup grated coconut
2 tablespoons bourbon whiskey or brandy

Combine egg yolks, sugar, and butter in a 2-quart saucepan. Cook over medium heat, stirring constantly, about 20 minutes or until thickened.

Remove from heat, and stir in remaining ingredients. Let cool before spreading on cake. Yield: enough for one 3-layer cake.

Frosting:

½ cup sugar
¼ cup light corn syrup
2 tablespoons water
⅛ teaspoon salt
2 egg whites
½ teaspoon vanilla extract

Combine sugar, syrup, water, and salt in a heavy saucepan. Cook over medium heat, stirring constantly, until mixture is clear. Cook, stirring frequently, until mixture reaches firm ball stage (242°).

Beat egg whites (at room temperature) until soft peaks form; continue beating egg whites while slowly adding syrup mixture. Add vanilla; continue beating until stiff peaks form and frosting is thick enough to spread. Yield: enough for one 3-layer cake.

Lane Cake, which originated in Alabama, is one of the South's most outstanding cakes. This showy creation has light, moist layers separated by fruit and nut-rich filling, covered with frosting reminiscent of divinity.

Unloading coconuts, Mobile docks, c.1895

ROCKY MOUNTAIN COCONUT CAKE

1 cup butter or margarine,
  softened
2 cups sugar
4 eggs
3 cups all-purpose flour
1 tablespoon baking powder
¼ teaspoon salt
1 cup milk
1 teaspoon vanilla extract
Rocky Mountain Filling
1 cup grated coconut

Cream butter; gradually add sugar, beating well. Add eggs, one at a time, beating well after each addition.

Combine flour, baking powder, and salt; add to creamed mixture alternately with milk, beginning and ending with flour mixture. Mix well after each addition. Stir in vanilla.

Pour batter into 3 greased and floured 9-inch round cakepans. Bake at 350° for 25 minutes or until a wooden pick inserted in center comes out clean. Cool in pans 10 minutes; remove layers from pans, and let cake cool completely.

Spread Rocky Mountain Filling between layers, and top with coconut. Yield: one 3-layer cake.

Rocky Mountain Filling:

1½ cups sugar
½ cup water
2 egg whites
2½ cups grated coconut
2 cups chopped raisins
1 cup currants
1 cup chopped blanched
  almonds

Combine sugar and water in a heavy saucepan. Cook over medium heat, stirring frequently, until mixture comes to a boil and sugar is dissolved.

Beat egg whites (at room temperature) until foamy. While beating at medium speed of electric mixer, slowly pour hot syrup in a thin stream over egg whites. Turn mixer to high speed, and continue beating until stiff peaks form and mixture is thick enough to spread. Stir in coconut, raisins, currants, and almonds. Yield: enough for one 3-layer cake.

Texas artist Seymour Thomas' oil painting of Sam Houston, 1893. Painted for the Chicago World's Fair.

SAM HOUSTON WHITE CAKE

¾ cup butter or margarine,
   softened
2 cups sugar
3 cups all-purpose flour
1 tablespoon baking
   powder
½ teaspoon salt
½ cup milk
½ cup water
1 teaspoon vanilla extract
½ teaspoon almond extract
6 egg whites
Chocolate Frosting

Cream butter; gradually add sugar, beating well.

Combine flour, baking powder, and salt. Combine milk and water. Add flour mixture to creamed mixture alternately with milk mixture, beginning and ending with flour mixture. Mix well after each addition. Stir in flavorings.

Beat egg whites (at room temperature) until stiff peaks form; fold into batter.

Pour batter into 3 greased and floured 9-inch round cakepans. Bake at 350° for 25 minutes or until a wooden pick inserted in the center comes out clean. Cool in pans 10 minutes; remove layers from pans, and let cool completely.

Spread Chocolate Frosting between layers and on top and sides of cooled cake. Yield: one 3-layer cake.

Chocolate Frosting:

3 (1-ounce) squares
   unsweetened chocolate
4 cups sifted powdered sugar
⅛ teaspoon salt
¼ cup hot water
3 egg yolks
¼ cup butter or margarine,
   melted
1 teaspoon vanilla
   extract

Place chocolate in top of a double boiler; place over boiling water and cook until melted.

Remove from heat; add sugar, salt, and hot water. Beat on medium speed of electric mixer until thoroughly blended. Add egg yolks, one at a time, beating well after each addition. Add butter and vanilla, beating until frosting reaches spreading consistency. Yield: enough for one 3-layer cake.

Of all the South's statesmen, Sam Houston may have been the most colorful and controversial. Born in Virginia in 1793, he moved to Tennessee as a child and was adopted by the Cherokees.

After serving in the Creek campaign, the tall, dramatic Houston served two terms in Congress. Adored by the public, he was elected Governor of Tennessee in 1827. When his wife left him, he resigned and spent six years among the Cherokees.

In 1836, as Commander-in-Chief of the Texas Provisional Government, he captured Santa Anna. He became President of the new Republic of Texas, then Senator when Texas became a state in 1845.

As Governor of Texas, he refused to side with the secessionists and was deposed in 1861. He retired to his farm until his death in 1863.

LA REINE CAKE (THE QUEEN)

1½ cups butter or margarine, softened
1½ cups sugar
3 eggs
2¼ cups sifted cake flour
2 teaspoons baking powder
½ teaspoon salt
½ cup plus 3 tablespoons milk
1 teaspoon vanilla extract
Frosting (recipe follows)
Fresh grated coconut (optional)

Cream butter in a large mixing bowl; gradually add sugar, beating until light and fluffy. Add eggs, one at a time, beating well after each addition.

Combine flour, baking powder, and salt; add to creamed mixture alternately with milk, beginning and ending with flour mixture. Stir in vanilla.

Pour batter into 3 greased and floured 9-inch round cakepans. Bake at 350° for 25 minutes or until a wooden pick inserted in center comes out clean. Cool in pans 10 minutes; remove from pans, and cool completely.

Spread frosting between layers and on top and sides of cooled cake. Sprinkle top and sides of frosted cake with grated coconut, if desired. Yield: one 3-layer cake.

Frosting:

2 cups sugar
2 egg whites
⅛ teaspoon cream of tartar
⅛ teaspoon salt
¼ cup plus 2 tablespoons water
1 teaspoon vanilla extract

Combine sugar, egg whites (at room temperature), cream of tartar, and salt in top of a large double boiler; add water, and beat on low speed of an electric mixer for 30 seconds or just until blended.

Place over boiling water; beat constantly on high speed of electric mixer about 7 minutes or until stiff peaks form. Remove from heat. Add vanilla; beat until frosting is thick enough to spread. Yield: enough for one 3-layer cake.

Lieutenant and Mrs. Robert E. Lee in 1838. From the portraits by William E. West.

GENERAL ROBERT E. LEE CAKE

2 cups all-purpose flour
½ teaspoon cream of tartar
1½ teaspoons baking powder
8 eggs, separated
2 cups sugar
2 teaspoons grated lemon rind
2 tablespoons lemon juice
Dash of salt
Lemon Jelly Filling
Lemon-Orange Frosting
¼ cup flaked coconut

Sift together first 3 ingredients; set aside. Beat egg yolks in a large mixing bowl until thick and lemon colored; gradually add sugar, beating well after each addition. Stir in lemon rind and juice.

Combine egg whites (at room temperature) and salt; beat until soft peaks form. Fold into egg yolk mixture alternately with flour mixture.

Spoon batter into 2 greased and floured 9-inch round cakepans. Bake at 325° for 25 to 30 minutes or until a wooden pick inserted in center comes out clean. Cool in pans 10 minutes; remove layers from pans, and let cool completely. Split layers horizontally.

Spread Lemon Jelly Filling between layers. Chill 30 minutes. Spread top and sides of cake with Lemon-Orange Frosting, and sprinkle with coconut. Yield: one 4-layer cake.

Arlington House, Virginia

Lemon Jelly Filling:

4 egg yolks
1⅓ cups sugar
2½ teaspoons grated lemon rind
¼ cup plus 1½ tablespoons lemon juice
¼ cup butter or margarine

Combine first 4 ingredients in top of a double boiler. Cook over high heat, stirring constantly, until sugar dissolves.

Add butter, and cook 20 minutes, stirring constantly, or until mixture is smooth and thickened. Cool filling thoroughly. Yield: enough for one 4-layer cake.

Lemon-Orange Frosting:

⅓ cup butter or margarine, softened
4 cups sifted powdered sugar
3 tablespoons grated orange rind
2½ tablespoons orange juice
1½ teaspoons grated lemon rind
1 tablespoon plus 1 teaspoon lemon juice
½ cup flaked coconut

Cream butter until light and fluffy. Add next 5 ingredients, beating until smooth. Stir in coconut. Yield: enough for one 4-layer cake.

MINNEHAHA CAKE

1 cup butter, softened
2 cups sugar
4 eggs, separated
3 cups all-purpose flour
1 tablespoon baking powder
Pinch of salt
1 cup milk
1½ teaspoons almond extract
Frosting (recipe follows)

Cream butter; gradually add sugar, beating well. Add egg yolks, one at a time, beating well after each addition.

Combine flour, baking powder, and salt; add to creamed mixture alternately with milk, beginning and ending with flour mixture. Mix well after each addition. Stir in flavoring.

Beat egg whites (at room temperature) until stiff peaks form; fold into batter.

Spoon batter into 2 greased and floured 8-inch square pans. Bake at 350° for 45 minutes or until cake tests done. Cool in pans 10 minutes; remove layers from pans, and let cool completely. Spread frosting between layers and on top and sides of cake. Yield: one 2-layer cake.

Frosting:

1½ cups sugar
2 egg whites
1½ teaspoons light corn syrup
¼ cup plus 1 tablespoon water
¼ teaspoon cream of tartar
1 cup raisins, chopped
1 cup chopped pecans
½ cup flaked coconut
1 teaspoon vanilla extract
½ teaspoon almond extract

Combine sugar, egg whites, and corn syrup in top of a large double boiler; add water and cream of tartar. Beat on low speed of electric mixer for 30 seconds or just until blended.

Place over boiling water; beat constantly on high speed of electric mixer about 7 minutes or until stiff peaks form. Remove from heat, and stir in remaining ingredients. Yield: enough for one 2-layer cake.

Hiawatha's Wedding Journey, *by J.L.G. Ferris, from* The Song of Hiawatha, *by Henry Wadsworth Longfellow.*

The New York Public Library Picture Collection

According to tradition, the dining room at Arlington was the locale for a marriage proposal. When Mary Custis kneeled to serve Lt. Robert E. Lee a piece of cake, he asked the question. The marriage in 1831 was a merging of two of Virginia's notable families. He was the son of Henry "Lighthorse Harry" Lee, she the great-granddaughter of Martha Washington.

DOLLY VARDEN CAKE

1 cup plus 3 tablespoons
  butter or margarine, divided
  and softened
2½ cups sugar, divided
4 cups all-purpose flour,
  divided
1 teaspoon baking
  powder
Pinch of salt
1 cup milk, divided
1 teaspoon vanilla
  extract
4 eggs, separated
3 egg yolks (reserve whites
  for frosting)
½ teaspoon ground
  cardamom
3 cups raisins, chopped
Frosting (recipe follows)

Grease and flour four 8-inch round cakepans; set aside.

Cream ½ cup butter in a large mixing bowl; gradually add 1 cup sugar, beating well.

Combine 2 cups flour, baking powder, and salt; add to creamed mixture alternately with ½ cup milk, beginning and ending with flour mixture. Stir in vanilla.

Beat 4 egg whites (at room temperature) until soft peaks form. Gently fold whites into batter. Set aside.

Cream remaining butter; gradually add remaining sugar, beating well. Add 7 egg yolks, one at a time, beating well after each addition.

Combine remaining flour and cardamom; add to creamed yolk mixture alternately with remaining milk, beginning and ending with flour mixture. Mix well after each addition. Add raisins, and stir well.

Pour egg white batter into 2 prepared cakepans. Pour yolk batter into remaining prepared cakepans. Bake at 350° for 30 to 35 minutes or until a wooden pick inserted in center comes out clean. Cool in pans 10 minutes; remove layers from pans, and cool completely.

Spread frosting between alternating yellow and white layers and on top and sides of cake. Yield: one 4-layer cake.

Dolly Varden, heroine of Dickens' *Barnaby Rudge*, lived in the cleanest house on the cleanest street in Clerkenwell with her father, Gabriel, a locksmith, and her mother, a spoiled, demanding woman. The house contained the shop and the dwelling, having been constructed of wood and plaster, "not planned with a dull and wearisome regard to regularity, for no one window matched the other. . . ."

Gabriel looks up toward his daughter's bedroom window: ". . . a roguish face met his; a face lighted up by the loveliest pair of sparkling eyes that ever a locksmith looked upon; the face of a pretty, laughing girl; dimpled and fresh, and healthful, the very impersonation of good-humour and beauty."

In the breakfast scene above, we see "the locksmith's rosy daughter, before whose dark eyes even beef grew insignificant, and malt became as nothing." Gabriel, grasping his Toby mug, has just mentioned Joe Willet, the object of her affection, and Dolly has fallen into a fit of embarrassed coughing.

Frosting:

2¼ cups sugar
3 egg whites
1½ tablespoons light corn
  syrup
Dash of salt
½ cup cold water
1½ teaspoons almond extract

Combine sugar, egg whites, corn syrup, and salt in top of a large double boiler; add cold water, and beat on low speed of electric mixer for 30 seconds.

Place over boiling water; beat constantly on high speed about 7 minutes or until stiff peaks form. Remove from heat. Add almond extract; beat 2 minutes or until frosting is thick enough to spread. Yield: enough for one 4-layer cake.

WILLIAMSBURG ORANGE CAKE

2½ cups all-purpose flour
1½ cups sugar
1½ teaspoons baking soda
¼ teaspoon salt
1½ cups buttermilk
½ cup butter or margarine, softened
¼ cup shortening
3 eggs
1½ teaspoons vanilla extract
1 tablespoon grated orange rind
1 cup golden raisins, chopped
½ cup finely chopped pecans
Williamsburg Butter Frosting
Orange rind and sections

Combine first 10 ingredients. Blend with an electric mixer 30 seconds on low speed; beat 3 minutes on high speed. Stir in raisins and pecans.

Pour into 3 greased and floured 8-inch round cakepans. Bake at 350° for 30 to 35 minutes or until a wooden pick inserted in center comes out clean. Cool in pans 10 minutes; remove from pans, and cool completely. Spread Williamsburg Butter Frosting between layers and on top and sides of cake. Garnish cake with orange rind and sections. Yield: one 3-layer cake.

Williamsburg Butter Frosting:

½ cup butter or margarine, softened
4½ cups sifted powdered sugar
1 tablespoon grated orange rind
4 to 5 tablespoons orange juice

Cream butter; gradually add sugar, beating well. Add orange rind and juice; beat until smooth. Yield: enough for one 3-layer cake.

Williamsburg Orange Cake is named for the South's exquisite gem situated between the York and James Rivers. Restored as a national monument, the city still endures.

WHITE MOUNTAIN CAKE

½ cup butter or margarine, softened
2 cups sugar
2½ cups all-purpose flour
2½ teaspoons baking powder
½ cup milk
8 egg whites
Frosting (recipe follows)
3 cups grated coconut, divided

Cream butter; gradually add sugar, beating well.

Combine flour and baking powder; add to creamed mixture alternately with milk, beginning and ending with flour mixture. Mix well after each addition. Beat egg whites (at room temperature) until stiff peaks form; fold into batter.

Pour batter into 3 greased and floured 9-inch round cakepans. Bake at 375° for 15 minutes or until a wooden pick inserted in center comes out clean. Cool in pans 10 minutes; remove from pans, and cool completely.

Spread frosting between layers, and sprinkle each with ¾ cup grated coconut. Spread remaining frosting on top and sides of cake and sprinkle with remaining coconut. Refrigerate until serving time. Yield: one 3-layer cake.

Frosting:

1½ cups sugar
2 egg whites
1 tablespoon light corn syrup
Dash of salt
⅓ cup cold water
1 teaspoon vanilla extract

Combine sugar, egg whites, syrup, and salt in top of a large double boiler; add cold water, and beat on low speed of electric mixer for 30 seconds or until just blended.

Place over boiling water; beat constantly on high speed of electric mixer about 7 minutes or until stiff peaks form. Remove from heat. Add vanilla extract; beat 2 minutes or until frosting is thick enough to spread. Yield: enough for one 3-layer cake.

Photographer: Charles Walton

GENERATIONS OF CAKE BAKING

AMBROSIA CAKE

⅔ cup shortening
1¾ cups sugar
2½ cups sifted cake flour
1 tablespoon baking powder
½ teaspoon salt
1 cup milk
1 cup flaked coconut
1½ teaspoons vanilla extract
5 egg whites
Orange Coconut Filling
White Frosting

Cream shortening; gradually add sugar, beating well.

Combine flour, baking powder, and salt; add to creamed mixture alternately with milk, beginning and ending with flour mixture. Stir in coconut and vanilla.

Beat egg whites (at room temperature) until soft peaks form; fold into batter.

Spoon batter into 2 greased and floured 9-inch round cakepans. Bake at 350° for 35 minutes or until a wooden pick inserted in center comes out clean. Cool in pans 10 minutes;

remove layers from pans, and let cool completely. Spread Orange Coconut Filling between layers; spread top and sides of cake with White Frosting. Yield: one 2-layer cake.

Orange Coconut Filling:

½ cup sugar
1½ teaspoons cornstarch
1 tablespoon butter or margarine
1 egg yolk, well beaten
⅓ cup flaked coconut
2 tablespoons grated orange rind
1 tablespoon orange juice
1 tablespoon lemon juice

Combine sugar, cornstarch, butter, egg yolk, and coconut in a heavy saucepan. Cook over medium heat, stirring constantly, until mixture thickens.

Remove from heat, and stir in orange rind and fruit juices. Cool. Yield: about 1½ cups.

White Frosting:

1 cup sugar
½ cup light corn syrup
¼ cup water
2 egg whites
1 teaspoon almond extract

Combine sugar, syrup, and water in a medium-size heavy saucepan. Cook over medium heat, stirring frequently, until mixture comes to a boil and sugar is dissolved. Continue cooking, stirring frequently, until mixture reaches soft ball stage (240°).

Beat egg whites (at room temperature) until foamy. While beating at medium speed of electric mixer, slowly pour hot syrup in a thin stream over egg whites. Turn mixer to high speed, and continue beating until stiff peaks form and frosting is thick enough to spread. Add almond extract; beat until blended. Yield: enough for one 2-layer cake.

DELICIOUS BANANA LAYER CAKE

½ cup butter or margarine, softened
1½ cups sugar
2 eggs, separated
1 teaspoon baking soda
¼ cup plus 1 tablespoon buttermilk
2 cups all-purpose flour
3 large ripe bananas, mashed
1 cup chopped pecans
Caramel Frosting

Cream butter; gradually add sugar, beating well. Add egg yolks, one at a time, beating well after each addition.

Dissolve soda in buttermilk; add to creamed mixture alternately with flour, beginning and ending with flour. Stir in mashed bananas and pecans.

Beat egg whites (at room temperature) until stiff peaks form; fold into batter.

Pour batter into 2 greased and floured 8-inch round cakepans. Bake at 350° for 30 minutes or until a wooden pick inserted in center comes out clean. Cool cake in pans 10 minutes; remove layers from pans, and let cool completely.

Spread Caramel Frosting between layers and on top and sides of cooled cake. Yield: one 2-layer cake.

Caramel Frosting:

1¼ cups sugar
¾ cup firmly packed brown sugar
About 1 cup evaporated milk
½ cup butter or margarine

Combine all ingredients in a heavy saucepan; cook over medium heat, stirring frequently, until mixture reaches soft ball stage (240°). Remove from heat, and beat until spreading consistency; add additional milk, if necessary. Spread immediately on cooled cake. Yield: enough for one 2-layer cake.

MOSS ROSE CAKE

3 cups grated coconut
1 tablespoon grated orange
  rind
2 tablespoons orange juice
2 tablespoons orange pulp
2 tablespoons sugar
4 eggs
2 cups sugar
2 cups sifted cake flour
2 teaspoons baking powder
½ teaspoon salt
1 cup hot milk (140°)
½ teaspoon almond extract
Frosting (recipe follows)
Orange slices

Combine first 5 ingredients; stir well. Refrigerate overnight in an airtight container.

Combine eggs in a large mixing bowl, beating 5 minutes or until thick and lemon colored. Gradually add sugar, beating until thick.

Sift flour, baking powder, and salt together; add to egg mixture alternately with hot milk. Beat well after each addition. Stir in flavoring.

Pour batter into 3 waxed paper-lined and greased 8-inch round cakepans. Bake at 350° for 20 minutes or until a wooden pick inserted in center comes out clean. Cool layers in pans 10 minutes; remove from pans, and let cool completely.

Spread frosting between layers, and sprinkle each with ¾ cup coconut-orange mixture. Spread remaining frosting on top and sides of cake. Top with remaining coconut-orange mixture, and garnish with orange slices. Refrigerate until serving time. Yield: one 3-layer cake.

Frosting:

1½ cups sugar
½ cup water
2 egg whites
1 teaspoon vanilla extract

Combine sugar and water in a saucepan. Cook over medium heat, stirring frequently, until mixture boils and sugar dissolves. Cook, stirring frequently, until mixture reaches soft ball stage (240°).

Beat egg whites (at room temperature) until foamy. While beating at medium speed of electric mixer, slowly pour hot syrup in a thin stream over egg whites. Turn mixer to high speed, and continue beating until stiff peaks form and frosting is thick enough to spread. Stir in vanilla; beat just until blended. Yield: enough for one 3-layer cake.

Moss Rose Cake and Delicious Banana Layer Cake. The Moss Rose is like an Ambrosia Cake in reverse: the orange-coconut mixture is in the layers instead of the frosting. Banana Cake is topped with rich caramel.

No. 94 **Cream City** 9-Inch Size
CHECKER BOARD CAKE PAN SET

The cakepan set came with recipe printed on the carton.

CHECKERBOARD CAKE

1 cup shortening
2 cups sugar
4 eggs, separated
3 cups sifted cake flour
1 tablespoon plus 1 teaspoon
  baking powder
1 teaspoon salt
1 cup milk
2 teaspoons vanilla extract
3 (1-ounce) squares
  semisweet chocolate,
  melted
Chocolate Butter Frosting

Cream shortening; gradually add sugar, beating well. Add egg yolks, one at a time, beating well after each addition.

Combine flour, baking powder, and salt; add to creamed mixture alternately with milk, beginning and ending with flour mixture. Mix well after each addition. Stir in vanilla.

Beat egg whites (at room temperature) until stiff peaks form; fold into batter.

Divide batter in half. Add melted chocolate to one-half of batter; mix well.

Line three 9-inch round checkerboard cakepans with greased waxed paper; grease sides of pan. Place checkerboard divider rings into one prepared pan. Spoon one-third of chocolate batter into center and outer rings; spoon one-third of white batter into middle ring, filling half full (a pastry bag may be used to pipe batters into rings). Smooth batter with a small spatula. Carefully remove checkerboard rings. Rinse rings and dry thoroughly before placing in next pan. Repeat procedure with second pan.

Spoon white batter into the center and outer rings of third pan, filling half full; spoon chocolate batter into middle ring, filling half full.

Bake at 350° for 20 minutes or until a wooden pick inserted in center comes out clean. Cool the layers in pans 10 minutes; remove layers from pans, and let cool completely.

Spread Chocolate Butter Frosting between layers, placing the white outer layer in the center. Frost top and sides of cake with remaining frosting. Yield: one 3-layer cake.

Chocolate Butter Frosting:

¼ cup plus 2 tablespoons
  butter or margarine
¼ cup plus 2 tablespoons
  milk
3 (1-ounce) squares
  semisweet chocolate
2 teaspoons almond extract
4 cups sifted powdered sugar

Combine butter, milk, and chocolate in top of a double boiler; place over boiling water, stirring constantly, until all ingredients are melted. Remove from heat, and stir in flavoring. Add sugar; beat until smooth and creamy. Yield: enough for one 3-layer cake.

JAPANESE FRUITCAKE

1 cup butter or margarine,
  softened
2 cups sugar
4 eggs
3 cups all-purpose flour
2 teaspoons baking powder
1 cup milk
1 teaspoon ground cinnamon
1 teaspoon ground cloves
1 teaspoon ground allspice
¾ cup chopped raisins
Coconut Filling
Cream Cheese Frosting
Chopped pecans

Grease and flour four 8-inch round cakepans. Set aside.

Cream butter; gradually add sugar, beating well. Add eggs, one at a time, beating well after each addition.

Combine flour and baking powder; add to creamed mixture alternately with milk, beginning and ending with flour mixture.

Spoon one-half of batter into 2 prepared cakepans. Combine spices and raisins; stir into remaining batter. Spoon into remaining prepared cakepans. Bake at 325° for 30 minutes or until a wooden pick inserted in center comes out clean. Cool in pans 10 minutes; remove layers from pans, and let cool completely. Spread Coconut Filling between layers of cooled cake; spread top and sides with Cream Cheese Frosting. Sprinkle cake with chopped pecans. Yield: one 4-layer cake.

Coconut Filling:

2 cups sugar
½ cup water
2 cups flaked coconut
1 tablespoon cornstarch
2 tablespoons cold water
1 tablespoon plus 1 teaspoon
  lemon rind
2 tablespoons lemon juice

Combine sugar, water, and coconut; cook over medium heat, until mixture boils. Dissolve cornstarch in cold water; stir into coconut mixture. Cook over low heat until mixture thickens. Remove from heat.

Add lemon rind and juice; stir well. Allow mixture to cool at room temperature. Yield: about 1½ cups.

Cream Cheese Frosting:

½ cup butter or margarine,
  softened
1 (8-ounce) package cream
  cheese, softened
1 (16-ounce) package
  powdered sugar, sifted
1 teaspoon vanilla extract

Combine butter and cream cheese, beating until light and fluffy. Add sugar and vanilla; beat until smooth. Yield: enough for one 4-layer cake.

Spice caddy, c.1882

CHOCOLATE RIBBON CAKE

¾ cup shortening
2¼ cups sugar
4½ cups all-purpose flour
1½ tablespoons baking
  powder
¾ teaspoon salt
1½ cups milk
1½ teaspoons vanilla
  extract
6 egg whites
5 (1-ounce) squares
  unsweetened chocolate,
  divided
1½ tablespoons plus 1
  teaspoon butter or
  margarine, divided
Marshmallow Frosting

Grease and flour three 9-inch round cakepans; set aside.

Cream shortening; gradually add sugar, beating well. Combine flour, baking powder, and salt; add to creamed mixture alternately with milk, beginning and ending with flour mixture. Beat well after each addition.

Beat egg whites (at room temperature) until stiff peaks form; gently fold into batter.

Pour one-third of batter into 1 prepared pan. Melt 3 squares chocolate and 1½ tablespoons butter; stir into remaining two-thirds batter. Pour into remaining prepared pans. Bake at 350° for 20 to 25 minutes or until a wooden pick inserted in center comes out clean. Cool in pans

10 minutes; remove from pans, and cool completely.

Spread Marshmallow Frosting between layers, placing white layer in the center. Frost top and sides of cake. Combine remaining chocolate and butter; melt over low heat, stirring frequently. Cool slightly, and drizzle over top of cake. Yield: one 3-layer cake.

Marshmallow Frosting:

1½ cups sugar
¾ cup water
¾ teaspoon vinegar
3 egg whites
15 large marshmallows,
  coarsely chopped

Combine first 3 ingredients in a heavy saucepan. Cook over medium heat, stirring frequently, until mixture comes to a boil and sugar dissolves. Continue cooking, stirring frequently, until mixture reaches soft ball stage (240°).

Beat egg whites (at room temperature) until foamy. While beating at medium speed of electric mixer, slowly pour hot syrup in a thin stream over egg whites. Turn mixer to high speed, and continue beating until stiff peaks form and frosting is thick enough to spread. Fold in marshmallows. Yield: enough for one 3-layer cake.

Farmer's Wife, *1925*

DEVIL'S FOOD CAKE

1¼ cups sugar, divided
¼ cup cocoa
1 cup milk, divided
1 egg yolk
½ cup shortening
2 eggs
2 cups sifted cake flour
¼ teaspoon salt
1 teaspoon baking soda
1 tablespoon hot water
1 teaspoon vanilla extract
Marshmallow Frosting

Combine ¼ cup sugar, cocoa, ½ cup milk, and 1 egg yolk in a saucepan. Cook over medium heat, stirring constantly, until thickened. Set aside.

Cream shortening; add remaining 1 cup sugar, beating well. Add eggs, one at a time, beating well after each addition.

Combine flour and salt; add to creamed mixture alternately with remaining milk, beginning and ending with flour mixture. Mix well after each addition. Add cocoa mixture; mix well.

Dissolve soda in hot water; add to creamed mixture. Mix well. Stir in vanilla.

Pour batter into 2 greased and floured 8-inch round cakepans. Bake at 350° for 20 minutes or until a wooden pick inserted in center comes out clean. Cool in pans 10 minutes. Remove from pans; cool completely. Spread frosting between layers and on top and sides of cake. Yield: one 2-layer cake.

Marshmallow Frosting:

1½ cups sugar
2 egg whites
1 tablespoon light corn syrup
¼ teaspoon cream of tartar
⅓ cup cold water
16 large marshmellows, quartered

Combine sugar, egg whites (at room temperature), syrup, and cream of tartar in the top of a large double boiler; add water, and beat on low speed of electric mixer for 30 seconds or just until blended.

Place over boiling water; beat constantly on high speed about 7 minutes or until stiff peaks form. Remove from heat, and add marshmallows. Continue beating until frosting is thick enough to spread. Yield: enough for one 2-layer cake.

GERMAN SWEET CHOCOLATE CAKE

1 (4-ounce) package sweet
 baking chocolate
½ cup boiling water
1 cup butter or margarine,
 softened
2 cups sugar
4 eggs, separated
1 teaspoon baking soda
1 cup buttermilk
2¼ cups all-purpose
 flour
½ teaspoon salt
1 teaspoon vanilla extract
Coconut-Pecan Filling

Combine chocolate and boiling water; stirring until melted. Set aside.

Cream butter; gradually add sugar, beating well. Add egg yolks, one at a time, beating well after each addition. Add chocolate mixture; beat well.

Dissolve soda in buttermilk. Combine flour and salt; add to creamed mixture alternately with buttermilk mixture, beginning and ending with flour mixture. Stir in vanilla.

Beat egg whites (at room temperature) until stiff peaks form; fold into batter.

Pour batter into 3 waxed paper-lined and greased 9-inch round cakepans. Bake at 350° for 30 minutes or until a wooden pick inserted in center comes out clean. Cool in pans 10 minutes; remove from pans, and cool completely.

Spread Coconut-Pecan Filling between the layers and on top of the cooled cake. Yield: one 3-layer cake.

Coconut-Pecan Filling:

1 cup whipping cream
1 cup sugar
3 egg yolks
½ cup butter or margarine
1 teaspoon vanilla
1⅓ cups flaked coconut
1 cup chopped pecans

Combine cream, sugar, egg yolks, and butter in a medium saucepan; cook over medium heat, stirring constantly, until thickened. Remove from heat, and stir in vanilla. Stir in remaining ingredients, and let cool completely. Yield: enough for one 3-layer cake.

German Chocolate Cake is somewhat of a misnomer. True, Walter Baker & Co., established in 1780, marketed a German sweet chocolate as "good to eat and good to drink." But Sam German, a coachman for Baker & Co., was responsible for developing German's Sweet Chocolate in 1852. Over 100 years later, the first published cake recipe appeared in a Dallas newspaper.

Collection of Bonnie Slotnick

CHOCOLATE YEAST CAKE

1 teaspoon dry yeast
¼ cup warm water (105°
 to 115°)
1 cup shortening
2 cups sugar
3 eggs
3 (1-ounce) squares
 unsweetened chocolate,
 melted
2¾ cups all-purpose flour
½ teaspoon salt
1 cup milk
1½ teaspoons vanilla
 extract
1 teaspoon soda
3 tablespoons hot water
Chocolate Icing

Dissolve yeast in warm water in a small bowl; set aside.

Cream shortening; gradually add sugar, beating well. Add eggs, one at a time, beating well

after each addition. Add melted chocolate; beat well.

Combine flour and salt; add to creamed mixture alternately with milk, beginning and ending with flour mixture. Mix well after each addition. Stir in yeast mixture and vanilla. Cover and refrigerate overnight.

Dissolve soda in hot water; add to refrigerated batter, and stir until well combined.

Pour batter into 3 greased and floured 8-inch cakepans. Bake at 350° for 25 minutes or until a wooden pick inserted in center comes out clean. Cool in pans 10 minutes; remove layers from pans, and let cool completely.

Spread Chocolate Icing between layers and on top and sides of cooled cake. Yield: one 3-layer cake.

Chocolate Icing:

¼ cup plus 2 tablespoons
 butter or margarine
¼ cup plus 2 tablespoons
 milk
3 (1-ounce) squares
 unsweetened chocolate,
 melted
⅛ teaspoon salt
1 tablespoon vanilla extract
About 4½ cups sifted
 powdered sugar

Combine butter, milk, and chocolate in top of double boiler; place over boiling water, stirring until mixture melts and is well blended. Remove from heat, and cool 10 minutes.

Stir in salt and vanilla. Gradually add sugar, beating to spreading consistency. Yield: enough for one 3-layer cake.

MAHOGANY CAKE

¾ cup butter or margarine,
  softened
2 cups firmly packed brown
  sugar
7 (1-ounce) squares
  semisweet chocolate,
  grated
½ cup boiling water
4 eggs
¾ teaspoon baking soda
½ cup buttermilk
3 cups all-purpose flour
1 teaspoon baking powder
1 teaspoon vanilla extract
Filling (recipe follows)
Sour Cream Chocolate
  Frosting

Combine butter, sugar, chocolate, and boiling water in a large mixing bowl; beat well. Add eggs, one at a time, beating well after each addition.

Dissolve soda in buttermilk; set aside. Combine flour and baking powder; add to chocolate mixture alternately with buttermilk mixture, beginning and ending with flour mixture. Mix well after each addition. Stir in the vanilla.

Pour batter into 2 greased and floured 9-inch round cakepans. Bake at 325° for 35 minutes or until a wooden pick inserted in center comes out clean. Cool in pans 10 minutes; remove the layers from pans, and let cool completely.

Spread the filling between layers; spread top and sides of the cooled cake with Sour Cream Chocolate Frosting. Yield: one 2-layer cake.

Illustration from A Thousand Ways to Please a Husband

Filling:

2 tablespoons butter or
  margarine
¾ cup firmly packed brown
  sugar
2 tablespoons plus 2
  teaspoons milk

Combine all ingredients in a small saucepan; cook over medium heat until mixture reaches soft ball stage (240°). Remove from heat, and beat until spreading consistency. Yield: about ½ cup.

Sour Cream Chocolate Frosting:

¼ cup butter or margarine,
  softened
3 (1-ounce) squares
  unsweetened chocolate,
  melted
2 cups sifted powdered sugar
½ cup sour cream
2 teaspoons vanilla extract

Combine all ingredients, beating until smooth. Yield: enough for one 2-layer cake.

Whether the recipe calls for sweet baking chocolate, unsweetened chunks, or cocoa, there are many who will take a chocolate cake in any form. Try Mahogany Cake for the darkest, and work through the Checkerboard to Mocha Layer Cake.

FIRST MYSTERY CAKE

½ cup shortening
1¼ cups sugar
2 eggs
2½ cups all-purpose flour
1 tablespoon plus 1 teaspoon
  baking powder
¼ teaspoon salt
½ teaspoon ground cinnamon
½ teaspoon ground nutmeg
1 cup milk
1 tablespoon cocoa
1 tablespoon boiling water
Creamy Mocha Icing

Grease and flour three 8-inch round cakepans; set aside.

Cream shortening; gradually add sugar, beating well. Add eggs, one at a time, beating well after each addition.

Combine flour, baking powder, salt, and spices; add to creamed mixture alternately with milk, beginning and ending with flour mixture. Mix well after each addition.

Pour two-thirds of batter into 2 prepared cakepans.

Dissolve cocoa in water; add to remaining one-third of batter, mixing well. Pour batter into remaining prepared cakepan. Bake layers at 375° for 15 minutes or until a wooden pick inserted in center comes out clean. Cool in pans 10 minutes; remove layers from pans, and let cool completely.

Spread Creamy Mocha Icing between layers, placing dark layer in the center. Frost top of cake with remaining frosting. Yield: one 3-layer cake.

Creamy Mocha Icing:

3 tablespoons butter or
  margarine, softened
1 (16-ounce) package
  powdered sugar, sifted
¼ cup plus 1 tablespoon
  cocoa
¼ cup plus 1 tablespoon
  strong coffee
1 teaspoon vanilla extract

Cream butter; add remaining ingredients, beating well. Yield: enough for one 3-layer cake.

MOCHA LAYER CAKE

1 cup butter or margarine,
  softened
2½ cups sugar
1 teaspoon baking soda
1 cup buttermilk
3 cups sifted cake flour
¼ teaspoon salt
¼ cup cocoa
1 tablespoon plus 2
  teaspoons strong coffee
2 teaspoons vanilla extract
5 egg whites
Mocha Frosting

Cream butter; gradually add sugar, beating well.

Dissolve soda in buttermilk. Combine flour, salt, and cocoa; add to creamed mixture alternately with buttermilk mixture, beginning and ending with flour mixture. Mix well after each addition. Stir in coffee and vanilla.

Beat egg whites (at room temperature) until stiff peaks form. Gently fold into the creamed mixture.

Pour into 3 greased and floured 8-inch round cakepans. Bake at 350° for 30 to 35 minutes or until a wooden pick inserted in center comes out clean. Cool in pans 10 minutes; remove from pans, and let cool completely.

Spread Mocha Frosting between layers and on top of cake. Yield: one 3-layer cake.

Mocha Frosting:

½ cup butter or margarine,
  softened
2 tablespoons cocoa
3 tablespoons strong coffee
1 egg yolk, beaten well
4½ cups sifted powdered
  sugar
2 teaspoons vanilla extract

Combine butter and cocoa; cream well. Add remaining ingredients, and beat until smooth. Yield: enough for one 3-layer cake.

Late 19th-century advertising card

MAYFLOWER GRAPE CAKE

½ cup shortening
1½ cups sugar
3 cups all-purpose flour
1 tablespoon baking powder
¾ teaspoon salt
½ cup milk
½ cup water
1½ teaspoons vanilla extract
4 egg whites
Grape Filling
Grape Frosting

Cream shortening; gradually add sugar, beating well.

Combine flour, baking powder, and salt; set aside. Combine milk and water. Add flour mixture to creamed mixture alternately with milk mixture, beginning and ending with flour mixture. Mix well after each addition. Stir in vanilla.

Beat egg whites (at room temperature) until stiff peaks form; fold into batter.

Pour batter into 2 greased and floured 9-inch round cakepans. Bake at 350° for 25 minutes or until a wooden pick inserted in center comes out clean. Cool in pans 10 to 15 minutes; remove layers from pans, and let cool completely.

Split each layer horizontally, and spread Grape Filling between layers, reserving ½ cup Grape Filling. Spread Grape Frosting on top and sides of cake. Drizzle top of cake with reserved Grape Filling. Yield: one 2-layer cake.

Grape Filling:

1 cup sugar
¼ cup plus 2 tablespoons cornstarch
½ teaspoon salt
1 cup grape juice
1 cup water
½ cup lemon juice
2 tablespoons butter or margarine

Combine sugar, cornstarch, salt, grape juice, and water in a medium saucepan, stirring well. Bring mixture to a boil over medium heat, and boil 1 minute, stirring constantly.

Remove from heat; add lemon juice and butter, stirring until well blended. Cool. Yield: about 2 cups.

Grape Frosting:

1½ cups sugar
2 egg whites
¼ cup plus 2 tablespoons grape juice
1 teaspoon corn syrup

Combine sugar, egg whites (at room temperature), grape juice, and syrup in the top of a large double boiler. Beat on low speed of electric mixer until well blended.

Place over boiling water; beat constantly on high speed about 7 minutes or until stiff peaks form. Remove from heat, and beat until frosting is thick enough to spread. Yield: enough for one 2-layer cake.

Mayflower Grape Cake: colorful and traditional

Embroidered picture featuring the "Mayflower," by Mississippian Ethel Wright Mohamed

TUTTI-FRUTTI CAKE

½ cup butter or margarine,
   softened
1 cup sugar
2 eggs
1½ cups all-purpose flour
2 tablespoons cocoa
1 teaspoon soda
½ cup buttermilk
½ cup chopped dates
½ cup chopped pecans
1 tablespoon vinegar
1 teaspoon vanilla
   extract
Tutti-Frutti Filling

Cream butter; gradually add sugar, beating well. Add eggs, one at a time, beating well after each addition.

Combine flour and cocoa in a medium mixing bowl. Dissolve soda in buttermilk, and add to creamed mixture alternately with flour mixture, beginning and ending with flour mixture. Mix well after each addition. Stir in dates, pecans, vinegar, and vanilla.

Pour batter into 2 greased and floured 8-inch round cakepans. Bake at 350° for 25 minutes or until a wooden pick inserted in center comes out clean. Cool in pans 10 minutes; remove layers from pans, and let cool completely. Spread Tutti-Frutti Filling between layers and on top of cake. Yield: one 2-layer cake.

Tutti-Frutti Filling:

1 cup sugar
1 (8-ounce) can crushed
   pineapple, drained
1 cup whipping cream,
   whipped

Combine sugar and drained pineapple in a heavy saucepan (reserve the pineapple juice for use in other recipes). Cook over medium heat until the mixture is very thick and pineapple is transparent. Cool mixture thoroughly.

Gently stir the cooled pineapple mixture into whipped cream. Yield: enough for one 2-layer cake.

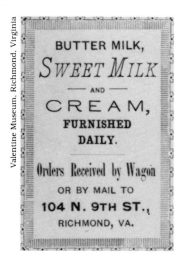

Above: Dairy receipt, 1887. Below: Renny Dairy, 1919, Richmond, Virginia.

WHIPPED CREAM CAKE

1 cup whipping cream
2 eggs
1 cup sugar
1½ cups all-purpose flour
2 teaspoons baking powder
½ teaspoon salt
1 teaspoon vanilla extract
1 cup whipping cream
2 tablespoons sugar
1 cup sliced fresh fruit (optional)

Beat 1 cup whipping cream until soft peaks form. Add eggs, one at a time, beating well after each addition. Gradually add sugar, beating well.

Combine the flour, baking powder, and salt, and fold into whipping cream mixture. Fold in vanilla.

Pour batter into 2 greased and floured 9-inch round cakepans. Bake at 375° for 15 minutes or until a wooden pick inserted in center comes out clean. Cool in pans 10 minutes; remove layers from pans, and let cake cool completely.

Beat 1 cup whipping cream until foamy; gradually add 2 tablespoons sugar, beating until soft peaks form. Spread sweetened whipped cream between layers and on top of cake. Top with fresh fruit, if desired. Yield: one 2-layer cake.

WHITE WONDER CAKE

½ cup shortening
1⅓ cups sugar
2¼ cups sifted cake flour
2½ teaspoons baking powder
½ teaspoon salt
1 cup milk
1 teaspoon vanilla extract
4 egg whites
Lemon Filling
Lemon Cream Frosting

Cream shortening; gradually add sugar, beating well. Combine flour, baking powder, and salt; add to creamed mixture alternately with milk, beginning and ending with flour mixture. Mix well after each addition. Stir in vanilla.

Beat egg whites (at room temperature) until stiff peaks form. Gently fold into batter.

Pour batter into 2 greased and floured 8-inch round cakepans. Bake at 375° for 20 to 25 minutes or until a wooden pick inserted in center comes out clean. Cool in pans 10 minutes; remove layers from pans, and let cool completely.

Spread Lemon Filling between layers; spread top and sides with Lemon Cream Frosting. Yield: one 2-layer cake.

Lemon Filling:

½ cup sugar
1½ tablespoons cornstarch
Dash of salt
½ cup cold water
1 egg yolk, slightly beaten
2 tablespoons lemon juice
½ teaspoon grated lemon rind
1½ teaspoons butter or
   margarine

Combine sugar, cornstarch, and salt in a medium saucepan, stirring well. Add water, egg yolk, and lemon juice; cook over medium heat, stirring constantly, until thickened. Remove from heat; stir in lemon rind and butter. Let cool. Yield: about 1 cup.

Lemon Cream Frosting:

½ cup butter, softened
2½ cups sifted powdered
   sugar
1 egg yolk
1 tablespoon whipping cream
1 tablespoon lemon juice
3 drops yellow food coloring

Cream butter; add remaining ingredients, beating until smooth. Yield: enough for one 2-layer cake.

WHITE AND YELLOW CAKE

¾ cup butter or margarine,
   softened
1½ cups sugar
3 cups sifted cake flour
1 tablespoon plus 1 teaspoon
   baking powder
1 teaspoon salt
1 cup milk
1 teaspoon vanilla extract
3 eggs, separated
3 drops yellow food coloring
Cream Filling
Cooked Cream Frosting

Grease and flour three 9-inch round cakepans; set aside.

Cream butter; gradually add sugar, beating well. Combine flour, baking powder, and salt; add to creamed mixture alternately with milk, beginning and ending with flour mixture. Mix well after each addition. Stir in vanilla.

Mix together one-third of batter, egg yolks, and food coloring; beat well, and set aside.

Beat egg whites (at room temperature) until stiff peaks form; gently fold into remaining two-thirds batter.

Pour yellow batter into 1 prepared cakepan. Pour white batter into remaining cakepans. Bake at 375° for 20 minutes or until a wooden pick inserted in center comes out clean. Cool in pans 10 minutes; remove layers from pan, and let cake cool completely.

Spread Cream Filling between layers, placing yellow layer in the center; spread top and sides with Cooked Cream Frosting. Yield: one 3-layer cake.

Cream Filling:

¼ cup sugar
1 tablespoon cornstarch
1 cup half-and-half
4 egg yolks, beaten
1½ teaspoons vanilla extract

Combine first 3 ingredients in top of a double boiler; place over boiling water. Cook 5 minutes, stirring constantly. Add egg yolks; cook, stirring until thickened. Remove from heat; stir in vanilla. Chill thoroughly. Yield: about 1 cup.

Cooked Cream Frosting:

1 cup half-and-half
1 cup sugar
3 egg yolks, beaten
1 tablespoon butter or
   margarine
1 cup finely chopped pecans
1 (3½-ounce) can flaked
   coconut

Combine half-and-half, sugar, and egg yolks in a medium saucepan; cook over medium heat until thickened. Add butter; stir well. Stir in pecans and coconut. Yield: enough for one 3-layer cake.

Egg label, c.1900

BOUNTIFUL HARVESTS

From winter's flood tide of citrus in our tropic South to succulent strawberries reddening in a northward wave in the spring, bounties are harvested and baked into seasonal treats from strawberry shortcake to dried apple stack cakes.

Georgia peaches hit the summer markets like an off-season Christmas present; figs ripen prodigally in Southern backyards, while the upper South laments the perishability that prevents their shipping for all to share. Native huckleberries, blackberries, and blueberries, both wild and cultivated, taunt us with seasons so short that to blink is to miss them completely.

Southerners know how to seize the moment to turn these fleeting gems of perfect ripeness into preserves and jams. How else would it be possible to serve a wedge of Heritage Jam Cake with Kentucky Fruit Filling or a generous square of Fig Preserves Cake with Buttermilk Candy Frosting on a chilly January day?

Autumn means pecans in the deeper South and black walnuts and hickory nuts further north. We learned their value from the native Americans, who depended heavily upon nuts for winter nourishment. Pecans were ground and made into a form of bread; the pioneers learned that as well.

Our forefathers kept walnuts and hickories by the hearth. Nearby were placed two goodly stones, the larger one slightly concave. Any member of the family with time to spend by the fire improved that time by cracking nuts for the family. Now, without bruising a finger, we can bake an opulent East Texas Hickory Nut Cake or a Black Walnut Spice Cake, thanks to mechanical "de-meating" machines.

The use of vegetables in cakes probably started as an economy measure. A cupful or two of pumpkin, sweet potatoes, carrots, or pinto beans makes a cheap bulking agent for large luscious cakes.

Apples are probably our most useful fruit for year-round use. Most apples grow best in the cooler, upper South. From early June apples to autumn-ripe Winesaps, these go straight into the batter for Auntie's Apple Cake or Nobby Apple Cake. And we dote on dried apples, which we cure by two or three methods. Taste one of our stack cakes; they're among our most satisfying Southern delicacies.

Spice is the common denominator in this trio of Southern beauties. Back to front: Apple Honey Upside-Down Cake (page 39), Black Walnut Spice Cake (page 50), and Pumpkin Cake (page 57), topped with a spicy whipped cream.

FROM ORCHARDS AND VINES

oses Coats, a Pennsylvania mechanic, was awarded the first recorded patent on an apple-paring gadget. His product, along with several hundred imitations and improvements, was eagerly snapped up by people desperate for help in the hard labor of drying fruit for winter.

In some parts of the country, neighbors would gather for an "apple bee," bringing their peelers along, to make short work of bushels of apples and, incidentally, to have a wonderful evening of fun. It was the custom in some places to thread the peeled and sliced apples on strings and hang them up to dry in a sunny place.

Another method for drying apples in quantity still in use today is this: Plan to dry fruit during warm, sunny weather. A pair of old window screens make ideal equipment. Pare, core, and slice fruit. Cover bottom screen with a clean cloth. Place fruit in a single layer on cloth and cover with the second screen to keep insects away.

Place in a sunny spot, such as a porch or even a low roof. Turn fruit daily and bring inside at night if heavy dew or rain is expected. Ten days to two weeks of hot, dry Texas weather will dry them, but it takes three or four weeks in the Appalachian regions.

When the process is complete, fruit should be dry and brown. Store in paper bags, tightly closed against insects, and hang in a dry place such as an attic. Peaches, pears, and apricots may also be prepared in this way.

Sulphured or "smoked" apples remain almost white, the time involved is greatly reduced, and many in the mountainous regions prefer them to the sun-dried variety.

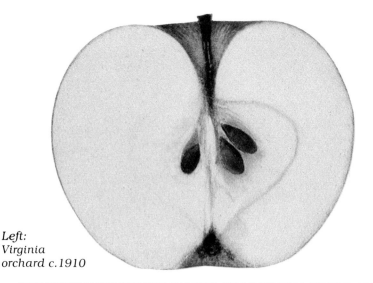

Left:
Virginia
orchard c.1910

BROWN APPLESAUCE CAKE

1 cup butter or margarine, softened
2 cups firmly packed brown sugar
1 egg
3 cups all-purpose flour, divided
2 teaspoons baking soda
¼ teaspoon salt
1 teaspoon ground cinnamon
1 teaspoon ground nutmeg
1 teaspoon ground cloves
2 cups applesauce
2 cups raisins
1 cup chopped black walnuts
Brandied Hard Sauce

Cream butter in large mixing bowl; gradually add brown sugar, beating until light and fluffy. Add egg, beating well.

Combine 2½ cups flour, soda, salt, and spices; add to creamed mixture alternately with applesauce, beginning and ending with flour mixture. Beat well after each addition.

Dredge raisins and black walnuts in remaining ½ cup flour; fold into batter. Pour batter into a greased and floured 10-inch tube pan. Bake at 350° for 1 hour and 15 minutes or until cake tests done. Cool in pan 15 minutes; remove from pan, and cool completely. Serve with Brandied Hard Sauce. Yield: one 10-inch cake.

Brandied Hard Sauce:

½ cup butter or margarine, softened
2 cups sifted powdered sugar
1 egg yolk, beaten
2 tablespoons brandy
½ teaspoon vanilla extract

Cream butter; gradually add sugar, beating until light and fluffy. Add remaining ingredients, mixing well. Yield: about 2 cups.

Dried Apple Cake is still a favorite in Kentucky.

DRIED APPLE CAKE

3 cups dried apples
1½ cups molasses
1 cup butter or margarine,
   softened
1½ cups sugar
2 eggs
1 teaspoon baking soda
1 cup buttermilk
4 cups all-purpose flour
2 teaspoons baking powder
1 teaspoon ground
   cinnamon
1 teaspoon ground cloves
1 teaspoon vanilla extract
1 cup raisins
1 cup chopped pecans
1½ cups peach preserves
1½ cups pear preserves

Soak dried apples in water to cover overnight. Drain well. Combine apples and molasses; cook over medium heat, stirring frequently, 20 minutes or until apples absorb molasses. Set aside.

Cream butter; gradually add sugar, beating until light and fluffy. Add eggs, one at a time, beating well after each addition. Set aside.

Dissolve soda in buttermilk, stirring well; set aside. Combine flour, baking powder, and spices; add to creamed mixture alternately with buttermilk mixture, beginning and ending with flour mixture. Mix well after each addition. Stir in apple mixture, vanilla, raisins, and pecans.

Pour batter into 3 greased and floured 9-inch round cakepans. Bake at 350° for 35 to 40 minutes or until a wooden pick inserted comes out clean. Cool in pans 10 minutes. Remove layers from pans; cool completely.

Combine peach and pear preserves, stirring well; spread between layers and on top of cake. Yield: one 3-layer cake.

DRIED APPLE FRUITCAKE

2 cups dried apples
1 cup molasses
1 cup butter or margarine,
   softened
1 cup sugar
2 eggs
2 teaspoons baking soda
1 cup buttermilk
4 cups all-purpose flour,
   divided
1 teaspoon ground cinnamon
¾ teaspoon ground allspice
¾ teaspoon ground cloves
½ teaspoon ground nutmeg
2 cups raisins
½ cup chopped candied citron
1 teaspoon vanilla extract
Whipped cream (optional)

Soak apples in cold water to cover overnight; drain well, and chop coarsely.

Combine chopped apples and molasses; cook over medium heat, stirring gently, about 30 minutes or until apples are tender and moisture is absorbed. Set aside.

Cream butter in a large mixing bowl; gradually add sugar, beating until light and fluffy. Add eggs, one at a time, beating well after each addition.

Dissolve soda in buttermilk. Combine 3½ cups flour with spices; mix well. Add flour mixture to creamed mixture alternately with buttermilk mixture, beginning and ending with flour mixture. Dredge raisins and citron in remaining ½ cup flour. Fold into batter. Stir in prepared apples and vanilla.

Pour batter into a waxed paper-lined and greased 13- x 9- x 2-inch baking pan. Bake at 300° for 1 hour and 15 minutes or until a wooden pick inserted in center comes out clean. Cool completely. To serve, cut into squares, and garnish each with a dollop of whipped cream, if desired. Yield: one dozen 3-inch squares.

AUNTIE'S APPLE CAKE

2 cups sugar
1½ cups vegetable oil
3 eggs
2 teaspoons vanilla extract
3 cups all-purpose flour,
   divided
1 teaspoon baking soda
1 teaspoon salt
1 teaspoon ground cinnamon
3 cups peeled, diced cooking
   apples
1 cup chopped pecans
Frosting (recipe follows)

Combine sugar, oil, eggs, and vanilla in a large mixing bowl; beat about 1 minute at medium speed of electric mixer. Combine 2½ cups flour, soda, salt, and cinnamon; gradually add to sugar mixture, beating at low speed of electric mixer until blended.

Dredge apples and pecans in remaining ½ cup flour; fold into batter. Spoon batter into a greased and floured 10-inch tube pan. Bake at 325° for 1 hour and 30 minutes or until wooden pick inserted in center comes out clean. Cool in pan 15 minutes; remove from pan, and let cool completely. Spread frosting over top of cake. Yield: one 10-inch cake.

Frosting:

1 cup firmly packed brown
   sugar
½ cup butter or margarine
¼ cup evaporated milk

Combine all ingredients in a medium saucepan; cook over medium heat, stirring frequently, until mixture comes to a boil and sugar is dissolved. Continue cooking, stirring constantly, until mixture reaches soft ball stage (240°). Remove from heat, and beat about 5 minutes or until thick enough to spread. Yield: enough for one 10-inch cake.

Peeling apples was sheer drudgery until Moses Coats patented the first mechanical apple parer.

APPLE HONEY UPSIDE-DOWN CAKE

2 tablespoons butter or
   margarine
½ cup firmly packed brown
   sugar
1 large cooking apple, peeled,
   cored, and cut into ½-inch
   rings
4 maraschino cherries,
   drained and halved
½ cup butter or margarine,
   softened
¾ cup honey
1 egg, beaten
¼ teaspoon baking soda
½ cup buttermilk
1½ cups all-purpose flour
1 teaspoon baking powder
1 teaspoon pumpkin pie spice
Whipped cream (optional)

Melt 2 tablespoons butter in a 9-inch cast-iron skillet. Spread brown sugar evenly over butter, and arrange apple rings on top of sugar. Place a cherry half in the center of each apple ring. Set aside.

Cream ½ cup butter and honey, beating until smooth. Add egg; mix well.

Dissolve soda in buttermilk. Combine flour, baking powder, and pumpkin pie spice; add to creamed mixture alternately with buttermilk mixture, beginning and ending with flour mixture. Beat well after each addition.

Spoon batter evenly over apple rings in skillet. Bake at 350° for 45 minutes or until a wooden pick inserted in center comes out clean. Cool 5 minutes, and carefully invert cake onto serving plate. Serve warm with whipped cream, if desired. Yield: one 9-inch cake.

Cornshucking Day at Tallyho, near Stem, Granville County, North Carolina, 1939. Dinner is topped off with a traditional stack cake.

NOBBY APPLE CAKE

3 tablespoons butter or
  margarine, softened
1 cup sugar
1 egg
1 cup plus 2 tablespoons
  all-purpose flour, divided
1 teaspoon baking powder
½ teaspoon salt
½ teaspoon ground nutmeg
½ teaspoon ground cinnamon
1 teaspoon vanilla extract
3 cups peeled, diced cooking
  apples
¼ cup chopped pecans
Whipped cream or ice cream
  (optional)

Cream butter; gradually add sugar, beating well. Add egg, beating well.

Combine ¾ cup flour, baking

A pple stack cake is at once the homeliest and the most toothsome of the South's favorite cakes. Native to the Appalachian Mountains where apples are most plentiful, the recipe includes molasses, ginger, or both. Nothing could be more "Southern" than our affinity for this flavor combination. Stack cake may be made from fresh applesauce or from cooked, dried apples. The latter is preferred by many for depth of flavor. The cake is definitely improved by a few days' aging.

In earlier days, the stack cake was used as a wedding cake. Guests would bring a layer and place it atop the layers already started on the plate. The taller the finished stack, the more popular, 'twas said, the bride. This feeling may have given rise to the advent of the footed cake stand. Even a three- or four-layer cake was thus made to look majestic.

powder, salt, and spices; add to creamed mixture, beating at low speed of electric mixer just until blended. Stir in vanilla (batter will be thick). Dredge apples and pecans in remaining ¼ cup plus 2 tablespoons flour; fold into batter.

Spoon batter into a greased and floured 8-inch square baking pan. Bake at 350° for 45 to 50 minutes or until a wooden pick inserted in center comes out clean. Serve warm with whipped cream or ice cream, if desired. Yield: one 8-inch cake.

MASSIE STACK CAKE

¾ cup shortening
1 cup sugar
1 cup molasses
3 eggs
4 cups all-purpose flour
½ teaspoon baking soda
1 teaspoon salt
1 teaspoon ground
  ginger
1 cup milk
3 cups applesauce
Ground cinnamon

Cream shortening; gradually add sugar and molasses, beating until smooth. Add eggs, one at a time, beating well after each addition.

Combine flour, soda, salt, and ginger; add to creamed mixture alternately with milk, beginning and ending with flour mixture. Beat well after each addition.

Spoon batter evenly into 6 greased and floured 9-inch round cakepans. Bake at 375° for 18 to 20 minutes or until a wooden pick inserted in center comes out clean. Carefully remove cake layers to the cooling racks.

Stack the cooled layers, spreading about ½ cup applesauce between each layer. Spoon remaining applesauce on top of cake. Sprinkle top of cake with cinnamon. Let stand overnight before serving. Yield: one 9-inch stack cake.

Note: Flavor of stack cake is enhanced when stored for several days.

TENNESSEE STACK CAKE

½ cup shortening
1¼ cups sugar
½ cup plus 2 tablespoons
  buttermilk
¾ teaspoon baking soda
1 tablespoon baking powder
¼ teaspoon salt
1¾ teaspoons ground ginger
3¾ cups all-purpose flour
Filling (recipe follows)
Dried apple slices

Cream shortening; gradually add sugar, beating well. Add buttermilk, soda, baking powder, salt, and ginger; mix well. Add flour, about 1 cup at a time, beating at medium speed of heavy-duty electric mixer to make a stiff dough.

Divide dough into 5 equal portions, and place each on a greased cookie sheet; pat into a 9-inch circle. Bake at 400° for 6 to 8 minutes or until golden brown. Carefully remove layers to cooling rack.

Stack the layers, spreading ¾ cup filling between each. Let stand overnight. Garnish top of cake with dried apple slices before serving. Yield: one 9-inch stack cake.

Filling:

4 cups dried apples
2⅔ cups water
½ cup sugar

Combine apples and water in a large saucepan; bring to a boil. Reduce heat; simmer 30 minutes or until tender. Cool.

Mash apples slightly, and stir in sugar. Cool filling completely. Yield: 3¾ cups.

Note: Flavor of stack cake is enhanced when stored for several days.

Massie Stack Cake (front) and Tennessee Stack Cake (back)

Picking Blackberries on the Fourth of July *by M. L. O'Kelley*

Wild berries were a source of amazement to colonists. Captain John Smith, while exploring the James River, spoke of Indians ". . .in all places kindly treating us, daunsing and feasting us with Strawberries, Mulberries, Bread, Fish and other Countrie Provisions."

BLUEBERRY POUND CAKE

1 cup plus 2 tablespoons butter or margarine, divided
2¼ cups sugar, divided
4 eggs
1 teaspoon vanilla extract
3 cups all-purpose flour, divided
1 teaspoon baking powder
½ teaspoon salt
2 cups fresh blueberries or canned blueberries, well drained

Grease a 10-inch tube pan with 2 tablespoons butter. Sprinkle pan with ¼ cup sugar; set aside.

Cream remaining 1 cup butter; gradually add remaining 2 cups sugar, beating well. Add eggs, one at a time, beating well after each addition. Add vanilla; mix well.

Combine 2¾ cups flour, baking powder, and salt; gradually add to creamed mixture, beating until well blended. Dredge blueberries with remaining ¼ cup flour; stir to coat well. Fold blueberries into batter. Pour batter into prepared pan.

Bake at 350° for 1 hour and 15 minutes or until cake tests done. Cool in pan 10 minutes; remove cake from pan, and let cool completely. Yield: one 10-inch cake.

BLACKBERRY CAKE

2 (15-ounce) cans
  blackberries, undrained
½ cup all-purpose flour
1 cup butter or margarine,
  softened
2 cups sugar
4 eggs
2½ cups all-purpose flour
3 tablespoons cocoa
1 tablespoon plus 1 teaspoon
  baking soda
1 teaspoon ground allspice
1 teaspoon ground cinnamon
1 teaspoon ground cloves
1 teaspoon vanilla extract
Caramel Cream Frosting

Drain blackberries, reserving ½ cup juice. Dredge blackberries in ½ cup flour.

Combine butter and sugar in a large mixing bowl, beating well. Add eggs, one at a time, beating well after each addition.

Combine 2½ cups flour, cocoa, soda, and spices; add to creamed mixture alternately with blackberry juice, beginning and ending with flour mixture. Beat well after each addition. Stir in blackberries and vanilla.

Pour batter into 3 greased and floured 9-inch round cake pans. Bake at 350° for 30 to 35 minutes or until wooden pick inserted in center comes out clean. Cool in pans 10 minutes; remove layers from pans, and let cool completely. Spread Caramel Cream Frosting between layers and on top and sides of cake. Yield: one 3-layer cake.

Caramel Cream Frosting:

¾ cup butter or margarine,
  softened
6 cups sifted powdered sugar
1½ tablespoons cocoa
¼ cup plus 1 tablespoon
  strong coffee
1½ teaspoons vanilla extract

Cream butter. Combine sugar and cocoa; add to butter alternately with coffee and vanilla. Beat until smooth. Yield: enough for one 3-layer cake.

Note: 2 cups fresh blackberries plus ½ cup juice may be substituted for canned berries.

Huckleberry Cake (front) and Blackberry Cake (back)

HUCKLEBERRY CAKE

½ cup butter or margarine,
  softened
1 cup sugar
3 eggs
1½ cups all-purpose flour,
  divided
2 teaspoons baking powder
½ teaspoon ground nutmeg
½ teaspoon ground cinnamon
½ cup milk
1 teaspoon lemon juice
1 cup fresh huckleberries,
  washed and drained

Combine butter and sugar in a large mixing bowl; beat well. Add eggs, one at a time, beating well after each addition.

Combine 1 cup flour, baking powder, and spices; add to creamed mixture alternately with milk, beginning and ending with flour mixture. Stir in lemon juice. Dredge huckleberries in remaining ½ cup flour; gently fold into batter.

Spoon batter into a waxed paper-lined and greased 9- x 5- x 3-inch loafpan. Bake at 350° for 1 hour and 5 minutes or until a wooden pick inserted in center comes out clean. Cool in pan 10 minutes; serve warm. Yield: one 9-inch loaf.

"Chairs" peaches originated about 1880 in the orchard of Franklin Chairs, Anne Arundel County, Maryland.

SOUTH CAROLINA FRESH PEACH CAKE

2 cups all-purpose flour, divided
1 teaspoon baking soda
1 teaspoon salt
1 teaspoon ground cinnamon
3 eggs, well beaten
1¾ cups sugar
1 cup vegetable oil
2 cups sliced fresh peaches
½ cup chopped pecans
Whipped cream

Combine 1½ cups flour, soda, salt, and cinnamon; mix well, and set aside.

Combine eggs, sugar, and oil; beat until smooth. Add flour mixture; beat at low speed of electric mixer just until blended (batter will be thick).

Dredge peaches and pecans in remaining ½ cup flour; gently fold into batter.

Spoon batter into a greased and floured 13- x 9- x 2-inch baking pan. Bake at 375° for 50 minutes or until a wooden pick inserted in center comes out clean. Cool completely. Cut into squares to serve; garnish each square with a dollop of whipped cream. Yield: one dozen 3-inch squares.

PERSIMMON CAKE

3 cups all-purpose flour
2 cups sugar
1 teaspoon ground cinnamon
½ teaspoon salt
1 teaspoon soda
1 cup vegetable oil
3 eggs, slightly beaten
1½ cups persimmon pulp (about 1½ pints persimmons)
1 cup chopped walnuts
Powdered sugar

Combine first 9 ingredients, mixing well. Pour into a greased and floured 10-inch Bundt pan. Bake at 325° for 1 hour or until done. Remove from pan while warm. Dust with powdered sugar. Yield: one 10-inch cake.

FRESH FIG LAYER CAKE

⅓ cup butter, softened
1 cup sugar
1 egg
2 cups all-purpose flour, divided
⅓ teaspoon salt
2 teaspoons baking powder
1 cup milk
½ cup finely chopped fresh figs
Fresh Fig Filling

Cream butter; gradually add sugar, beating well. Add egg; beat well. Combine 1½ cups flour, salt, and baking powder; add to creamed mixture alternately with milk, beginning and ending with flour mixture, beating well after each addition. Dredge figs in remaining ½ cup flour; fold into batter.

Pour into 2 greased and floured 8-inch round cakepans. Bake at 350° for 35 minutes or until wooden pick inserted in center comes out clean. Cool in pans 10 minutes; remove layers from pans, and cool completely. Spread Fresh Fig Filling between layers and on top and sides of cooled cake. Yield: one 2-layer cake.

Fresh Fig Filling:

1 pound fresh figs, chopped
⅓ cup sugar
⅓ cup water
1 tablespoon lemon juice

Combine all ingredients in a medium saucepan; bring to a boil. Reduce heat to medium; cook 30 minutes or until thickened, stirring constantly. Yield: enough for one 2-layer cake.

Lemon fig

FIG PRESERVES CAKE

2 cups all-purpose flour
2 tablespoons cornstarch
1 teaspoon baking soda
¼ teaspoon salt
1 teaspoon ground cinnamon
1 teaspoon ground nutmeg
½ teaspoon ground cloves
3 eggs
1 cup vegetable oil
1 cup buttermilk
1½ cups sugar
1 tablespoon vanilla
  extract
1 cup
Fig preserves
½ cup chopped pecans
Buttermilk Candy Frosting

Combine flour, cornstarch, soda, salt, and spices; set aside.

Combine eggs, oil, buttermilk, sugar, and vanilla; beat until smooth. Stir in flour mixture, fig preserves, and pecans. Pour batter into a well-greased 13- x 9- x 2-inch baking pan.

Bake at 325° for 45 minutes or until a wooden pick inserted in center comes out clean.

Spread Buttermilk Candy Frosting over warm cake. Yield: one 13- x 9-inch cake.

Buttermilk Candy Frosting:

1 cup sugar
½ cup buttermilk
1 tablespoon light corn
  syrup
½ teaspoon baking soda
1 tablespoon butter, softened

Combine first 4 ingredients in a medium saucepan. Cook over medium heat, stirring frequently, until mixture comes to a boil. Boil 3 minutes or until syrup mixture reaches 220°, stirring constantly. Remove from heat, and stir in butter. Cool.

Beat on medium speed of electric mixer about 5 minutes or until thick enough to spread. Yield: enough for one 13- x 9-inch cake.

A time-honored custom: Putting up jellies and jams

HERITAGE JAM CAKE

1 cup butter or margarine,
  softened
2 cups sugar
5 eggs
1 teaspoon baking soda
1 cup buttermilk
3 cups flour, divided
¼ teaspoon salt
½ teaspoon ground
  cinnamon
1 teaspoon ground cloves
1 teaspoon allspice
1 cup chopped dates
1 cup chopped pecans
1 cup grape jam
Kentucky Fruit Filling

Cream butter; gradually add sugar, beating well. Add eggs, one at a time, beating well after each addition. Set aside.

Dissolve soda in buttermilk; stir well. Combine 2½ cups flour, salt, and spices; add to creamed mixture alternately with buttermilk mixture, beginning and ending with flour mixture. Combine dates and pecans; dredge in remaining flour. Fold into batter. Carefully fold grape jam into batter.

Pour batter into 2 waxed paper-lined and greased 9-inch round cakepans. Bake at 350° for 40 to 45 minutes or until a wooden pick inserted in center comes out clean. Cool in pans 10 minutes; remove layers from pans, and let cool completely.

Spread hot Kentucky Fruit Filling between layers and on top of cooled cake. Yield: one 2-layer cake.

Kentucky Fruit Filling:

1 cup chopped dates
1 cup raisins, chopped
1 orange, unpeeled, seeded,
  and ground
1 lemon, unpeeled, seeded,
  and ground
⅓ cup sugar
¼ cup orange juice

Combine first 4 ingredients in a medium saucepan; stir well. Add sugar and orange juice; cook over medium heat, stirring constantly, until mixture is thickened. Spread hot filling between layers and on top of cake. Yield: about 2 cups.

"LITTLE NANNY'S" BLACKBERRY JAM CAKE

1 tablespoon butter or
  margarine, softened
1 cup sugar
2 egg yolks
1 teaspoon baking soda
1 cup buttermilk
2 cups all-purpose flour
1 teaspoon baking powder
½ teaspoon salt
1 teaspoon cocoa
1 teaspoon ground cinnamon
½ teaspoon ground allspice
1 cup blackberry jam
Glaze (recipe follows)

Cream butter and sugar, beating well. Add egg yolks, beating mixture well.

Dissolve soda in buttermilk, stirring well; set aside. Combine flour, baking powder, salt, cocoa, cinnamon, and allspice; add to the creamed mixture alternately with the buttermilk mixture, beginning and ending with flour mixture. Fold in blackberry jam.

Pour batter into a greased and floured 10-inch Bundt pan. Bake at 350° for 45 to 50 minutes or until cake tests done. Cool in pan 15 minutes; remove from pan, and cool completely. Spoon glaze over top of cake. Yield: one 10-inch cake.

Glaze:

1 cup sifted powdered sugar
1 to 2 tablespoons milk
1 tablespoon butter or
  margarine, softened
½ teaspoon vanilla extract

Combine all ingredients, and beat until mixture is smooth. Yield: about ½ cup.

BROWN'S CHURCH JAM CAKE

1 teaspoon baking soda
¾ cup buttermilk
1 cup butter or margarine,
  softened
1½ cups sugar
4 eggs
2½ cups all-purpose flour
1 teaspoon pumpkin pie spice
1½ cups strawberry jam
Egg Nog Icing

Dissolve soda in buttermilk; stir well, and set aside.

Cream butter; gradually add sugar, beating until light and fluffy. Add eggs, one at a time, beating well after each addition. Set aside.

Combine flour and pumpkin pie spice; add to creamed mixture alternately with buttermilk mixture, beginning and ending with flour mixture. Fold jam into batter.

Pour batter into 3 waxed paper-lined and heavily greased 9-inch round cakepans. Bake at 350° for 40 to 50 minutes or until a wooden pick inserted in center comes out clean. Cool in pans 10 minutes; remove layers from pans, and let cake cool completely.

Spread Egg Nog Icing between layers and on top and sides of the cooled cake. Yield: one 3-layer cake.

Egg Nog Icing:

½ cup butter or margarine,
  softened
3 egg yolks
6 cups sifted powdered
  sugar
¼ cup bourbon whiskey

Combine butter and egg yolks; beat until smooth. Gradually add powdered sugar, 2 cups at a time, alternately with bourbon; beat well after each addition. Yield: enough for one 3-layer cake.

When a cake has been identified with a name for over a hundred years, somehow its meaning is intensified. Little Nanny (Emma Margaret Dodson Samuel) of Chattanooga, Tennessee, was famous for her cakes. She was expected to bring her Blackberry Jam Cake to any and all social functions.

The hospitable custom of "dinner on the grounds" lingers to this day and is the background of Brown's Church Jam Cake which originated in Tennessee.

Collection of Business Americana

Label from a can of blackberries from the late 19th century

Pear Preserves Cake has spiced layers frosted with caramel.

PEAR PRESERVES CAKE

1 cup butter, softened
2 cups sugar
5 eggs, separated
1 teaspoon baking soda
1 cup buttermilk
3 cups all-purpose flour,
   divided
1 teaspoon ground cinnamon
1 teaspoon ground allspice
1 teaspoon ground nutmeg
1 cup chopped pecans
1 cup pear preserves
Heritage Caramel Frosting

Cream butter in a large mixing bowl; gradually add sugar, beating until light and fluffy. Add egg yolks; beat well.

Dissolve soda in buttermilk; stir well. Combine 2½ cups flour and spices; add to creamed mixture alternately with buttermilk mixture, beginning and ending with flour mixture. Mix well after each addition.

Dredge pecans in remaining ½ cup flour; fold pecans and pear preserves into batter. Beat egg whites (at room temperature) until stiff peaks form; gently fold into batter.

Pour batter into 3 waxed paper-lined and heavily greased 9-inch round cakepans. Bake at 350° for 35 to 40 minutes, or until a wooden pick inserted in center comes out clean. Cool in pans 10 minutes; remove layers from pans, and let cake cool completely.

Spread Heritage Caramel Frosting between layers and on top and sides of cooled cake. Yield: one 3-layer cake.

Heritage Caramel Frosting:

4½ cups sugar, divided
1½ cups milk
¾ cup butter or margarine,
   softened

Combine 3 cups sugar and milk in a large saucepan; cook over low heat, stirring frequently, until sugar is dissolved. Remove from heat, and set aside.

Place remaining 1½ cups sugar in a 10-inch cast-iron skillet; cook over medium heat, stirring constantly, until sugar dissolves and becomes a golden syrup. Add butter, stirring well.

Gradually pour syrup mixture into reserved milk mixture in saucepan. Cook over medium heat, stirring constantly, until the mixture reaches soft ball stage (240°).

Remove from heat, and beat mixture at medium speed of electric mixer about 5 minutes or until thick enough to spread. Spread immediately on cooled cake. Yield: enough for one 3-layer cake.

Texas Pecan Cake

TEXAS PECAN CAKE

2 cups butter or margarine,
  softened
2 cups sugar
6 eggs
4 cups all-purpose flour,
  divided
1½ teaspoons baking powder
1 (2-ounce) bottle lemon
  extract
4 cups chopped pecans
2½ cups golden raisins

Cream butter in a large mixing bowl; gradually add sugar, beating until light and fluffy. Add eggs, one at a time, beating well after each addition.

Combine 3½ cups flour and baking powder; gradually add to creamed mixture alternately with lemon extract, beginning and ending with flour mixture. Beat well after each addition

(batter will be thick). Dredge pecans and raisins in remaining ½ cup flour; stir into batter.

Spoon batter into a greased and floured 10-inch tube pan. Bake at 325° for 1 hour and 30 minutes or until cake tests done. Cool in pan 15 minutes; remove, and let cool completely before serving. Yield: one 10-inch cake.

BRINGHURST PECAN CAKE

1 cup butter, softened
2 cups sugar
6 eggs
4 cups all-purpose flour,
  divided
1 teaspoon baking powder
1½ tablespoons grated
  nutmeg
1 cup bourbon whiskey
2½ cups raisins
2 cups chopped pecans

Cream butter in a large mixing bowl; gradually add sugar, beating well. Add eggs, one at a time, beating mixture well after each addition.

Combine 3¾ cups flour, baking powder, and nutmeg; add to creamed mixture alternately with bourbon, beginning and ending with flour mixture. Mix well after each addition.

Dredge raisins and pecans in remaining ¼ cup flour; stir into batter.

Spoon batter into a heavily greased 10-inch tube pan. Bake at 325° for 1 hour and 15 minutes or until cake tests done. Cool cake in pan 15 minutes; remove cake from pan, and let cool completely. Yield: one 10-inch cake.

LEMON PECAN CAKE

2 cups butter or margarine,
  softened
2¼ cups firmly packed brown
  sugar
6 eggs, separated
4 cups all-purpose flour
1¼ teaspoons baking powder
⅛ teaspoon salt
½ cup milk
2 tablespoons plus 2
  teaspoons lemon extract
1 pound pecans, chopped

Cream butter; gradually add
brown sugar, beating until light
and fluffy. Add egg yolks, one at
a time, beating well after each
addition.

Combine flour, baking powder, and salt; add to creamed
mixture alternately with milk,
beginning and ending with
flour mixture. Beat well after
each addition. Stir in lemon extract and pecans.

Beat egg whites (at room temperature) until stiff peaks form;
fold into batter.

Pour batter into a greased 10-
inch tube pan. Bake at 325° for
1 hour and 15 minutes or until
cake tests done. Cool in pan 15
minutes; remove from pan, and
cool completely. Yield: one 10-
inch cake.

Pecans

MAJOR

BURKETT

WARRICK

RAVENS

OWENS

PECAN UPSIDE-DOWN CAKE

3 tablespoons butter or
  margarine, melted
1 cup firmly packed brown
  sugar
¾ cup plus 1 tablespoon
  boiling water, divided
1 cup chopped pecans
2 eggs, separated
1 cup sugar
1 teaspoon vanilla extract
1 cup all-purpose flour
1½ teaspoons baking powder
½ teaspoon salt

Combine butter, brown
sugar, and 1 tablespoon boiling
water in a 9-inch round cakepan; stir well. Sprinkle pecans
evenly over top; set aside.

Beat egg yolks until thick and
lemon colored; add sugar and
vanilla, beating well. Combine
flour, baking powder, and salt;
add to yolk mixture alternately
with remaining ¾ cup boiling
water, beginning and ending
with flour mixture. Beat well
after each addition.

Beat egg whites (at room temperature) until soft peaks form;
gently fold into batter. Pour batter evenly over pecans in pan.
Bake at 325° for 35 mintes or
until wooden pick inserted in
center comes out clean. Cool in
pan 10 minutes. Invert cake
onto serving plate. Yield: one 9-
inch cake.

EAST TEXAS HICKORY NUT CAKE

½ cup butter or margarine,
  softened
1¼ cups sugar
2 eggs, separated
2 cups sifted cake flour
1 tablespoon baking
  powder
¼ teaspoon salt
¾ cup milk
2 teaspoons vanilla
  extract
Caramel Frosting
1 cup chopped hickory nuts
  or walnuts, divided

Cream butter in a large mixing bowl; gradually add sugar,
beating until light and fluffy.
Add egg yolks, one at a time,
beating well after each addition.

Combine flour, baking powder, and salt; add to creamed
mixture alternately with milk,
beginning and ending with
flour mixture. Mix well after
each addition. Stir in vanilla.

Pour batter into 2 greased and
floured 8-inch round cakepans.
Bake at 375° for 20 to 25 minutes or until a wooden pick inserted in center comes out
clean. Cool in pans 10 minutes;
remove layers from pans and
cool completely.

Spread Caramel Frosting between layers and sprinkle with
½ cup chopped nuts. Spread

top and sides with frosting, and
sprinkle with remaining ½ cup
nuts. Yield: one 2-layer cake.

Caramel Frosting:

¾ cup butter or margarine,
  softened
1½ cups sugar
¾ teaspoon baking
  soda
¾ cup buttermilk
½ teaspoon vanilla
  extract

Cream butter; gradually add
sugar, beating well with electric
mixer.

Dissolve soda in buttermilk.
Add to creamed mixture, beating well.

Cook mixture in large saucepan over medium heat, stirring
constantly, until mixture
reaches soft ball stage (240°).
Remove from heat, and add vanilla (do not stir); cool mixture
10 minutes.

Beat on medium speed of electric mixer about 10 minutes or
until thick enough to spread.
Spread immediately on cooled
cake. Yield: enough for one 2-
layer cake.

Note: One cup chopped
pecans may be substituted for
hickory nuts or walnuts in cake.

BLACK WALNUT
SPICE CAKE

1 cup chopped black
  walnuts
½ cup shortening
2 cups firmly packed
  brown sugar
3 eggs, separated
3 cups all-purpose flour,
  divided
1 tablespoon baking powder
½ teaspoon salt
½ teaspoon ground cinnamon
½ teaspoon ground nutmeg
½ teaspoon ground cloves
¾ cup milk
Buttery Cinnamon Frosting
Chopped walnuts

Place 1 cup chopped walnuts
in boiling water 3 to 5 minutes;
drain well, and set aside.

Cream shortening; gradually
add sugar, beating well. Add egg
yolks; beat well.

Combine 2¾ cups flour, baking powder, salt, and spices;
mix well. Add flour mixture to
creamed mixture alternately
with milk, beginning and ending with flour mixture. Mix well
after each addition. Dredge
black walnuts in remaining ¼
cup flour; fold into batter. Beat
egg whites (at room temperature) until stiff peaks form; fold
into batter.

Pour batter into 3 greased and
floured 8-inch square cakepans.
Bake at 350° for 25 to 30 minutes or until a wooden pick inserted in center comes out
clean. Cool in pans 10 minutes;
remove layers from pans, and let
cool completely. Spread Buttery
Cinnamon Frosting between
layers and on top and sides of
cake. Garnish with additional
chopped walnuts. Yield: one 3-
layer cake.

Buttery Cinnamon Frosting:

1 cup butter or margarine,
  softened
7½ cups sifted powdered
  sugar, divided
1¼ teaspoon ground
  cinnamon
⅛ teaspoon salt
¼ cup plus 1 tablespoon milk
2½ teaspoons vanilla extract

*In this photograph, taken
for the 1939 New York
World's Fair, men cluster
peanut vines about poles
for curing.*

Cream butter in a large mixing bowl. Combine 2 cups powdered sugar, cinnamon, and
salt; gradually add to butter,
beating with an electric mixer
until light and fluffy. Add remaining 5½ cups powdered
sugar alternately with milk,
beating until smooth. Add vanilla; beat well. Yield: enough
for one 3-layer cake.

ORANGE-WALNUT
CAKE

1 cup butter or margarine,
  softened
2 cups sugar
5 eggs, separated
3 cups all-purpose flour
1 tablespoon baking powder
2 teaspoons grated orange
  rind
½ teaspoon ground nutmeg
1 cup milk
1 cup chopped walnuts
Cream Cheese Frosting

Cream butter; gradually add
sugar, beating well. Add egg

HARVEST PEANUT CAKE

1 cup creamy peanut
  butter
⅔ cup butter or margarine,
  softened
2 cups firmly packed brown
  sugar
6 eggs
2 cups all-purpose flour
2 teaspoons baking powder
½ teaspoon salt
¾ cup milk
2 teaspoons vanilla
  extract
Peanut Butter Frosting
½ cup chopped roasted
  peanuts

Cream peanut butter and butter. Gradually add sugar, beating well. Add eggs, one at a time, beating well after each addition.

Combine flour, baking powder, and salt; add to creamed mixture alternately with milk, beating well after each addition. Stir in vanilla.

Pour batter into a greased and floured 13- x 9- x 2-inch baking pan. Bake at 350° for 45 to 50 minutes or until wooden pick inserted in center comes out clean. Cool cake in pan completely. Spread Peanut Butter Frosting on top of cake. Sprinkle with peanuts. Cut into squares to serve. Yield: one 13- x 9-inch cake.

Peanut Butter Frosting:

½ cup creamy peanut butter
1 (16-ounce) package
  powdered sugar, sifted
½ cup plus 1 tablespoon milk
1 teaspoon vanilla extract

Cream peanut butter; gradually add half of sugar, beating well. Add remaining sugar alternately with milk, beating until smooth enough to spread. Add vanilla; beat well. Yield: enough for one 13- x 9- inch cake.

yolks, one at a time, beating well after each addition.

Combine flour, baking powder, orange rind, and nutmeg; add to creamed mixture alternately with milk, beginning and ending with flour mixture. Stir in walnuts.

Beat egg whites (at room temperature) until stiff peaks form; gently fold into batter.

Pour batter into a greased and floured 13- x 9- x 2-inch baking pan. Bake at 350° for 45 to 50 minutes or until wooden pick inserted in center comes out clean. Cool completely; spread Cream Cheese Frosting on top

of cake. Cut cooled cake into squares to serve. Yield: one 13- x 9-inch cake.

Cream Cheese Frosting:

1 (8-ounce) package cream
  cheese, softened
2 tablespoons milk
1 (16-ounce) package
  powdered sugar, sifted
1 teaspoon vanilla
  extract

Beat cream cheese until light and fluffy; gradually add remaining ingredients, beating well. Yield: enough for one 13- x 9-inch cake.

SPRINGTIME SHORTCAKES

Strawberry Shortcake is one of the Rites of Spring in the South.

STRAWBERRY SHORTCAKE

1 quart fresh strawberries, sliced
½ cup sugar
2 cups all-purpose flour
1 tablespoon baking powder
2 tablespoons sugar
⅓ cup shortening
⅔ cup milk
2 tablespoons butter or margarine, melted
1 cup whipping cream, whipped
Whole strawberries

Combine sliced strawberries and ½ cup sugar; stir gently, and chill 1 to 2 hours.

Combine flour, baking powder, and 2 tablespoons sugar in a large mixing bowl; cut in shortening with pastry blender until mixture resembles coarse meal. Add milk to flour mixture; stir with a fork until a soft dough forms.

Divide dough in half. Pat each half out evenly in a greased and floured 8-inch cakepan. (Dough will be sticky; dust hands with flour as necessary.) Brush surface of each with 1 tablespoon melted butter. Bake at 450° for 15 minutes or until layers are golden brown. Cool on wire racks. (Layers will be thin.)

Place 1 cake layer on serving plate. Spoon on half of whipped cream, and arrange half of sliced strawberries on top. Repeat procedure with remaining cake, whipped cream, and strawberries, reserving small amount of whipped cream. Garnish top of cake with remaining whipped cream and whole strawberries. Yield: one 2-layer shortcake.

The Southerner's love affair with shortcake must have come quickly on the heels of his tribal craving for biscuits. Is there one among us who, sitting at a table with a hot, buttered biscuit on our plate, within sight of a bowl of sweetened berries and a pitcher of rich cream, would not have invented short-cake? Of course not.

OLD-FASHIONED STRAWBERRY SHORTCAKE

1 quart fresh strawberries, sliced
¼ cup sugar
2 cups all-purpose flour
¼ cup sugar
2 teaspoons baking powder
½ teaspoon salt
⅓ cup butter
¾ cup milk
1 egg
1 egg white
¼ cup butter, melted
1 cup whipping cream
¼ cup sifted powdered sugar
5 to 6 whole strawberries

Combine sliced strawberries and ¼ cup sugar; stir gently, and chill 1 to 2 hours.

Combine flour, ¼ cup sugar, baking powder, and salt in a large mixing bowl; cut in ⅓ cup butter until mixture resembles coarse meal.

Combine milk and whole egg; beat well. Add to flour mixture; stir with a fork until a soft dough forms. Pat half of dough out to ½-inch thickness in a greased and floured 9-inch round cakepan. (Dough will be sticky; dust hands with flour.)

Beat egg white, (at room temperature) until stiff but not dry. Brush surface of dough with half of beaten egg white and 1 tablespoon melted butter.

Roll out remaining dough to ½-inch thickness on a lightly floured surface. Place on top of layer in cakepan; trim excess pastry. Brush surface with remaining beaten egg white and 1 tablespoon melted butter.

Bake at 450° for 12 minutes. Remove from pan; while still warm split the two layers and spread each with 1 tablespoon melted butter.

Beat whipping cream until foamy; gradually add powdered sugar, beating until soft peaks form. Place 1 cake layer on serving plate. Spoon on half of whipped cream, and arrange half of sliced strawberries on top. Repeat procedure with remaining cake, whipped cream, and strawberries, reserving some whipped cream. Garnish top of cake with remaining whipped cream and whole strawberries. Yield: one 2-layer shortcake.

FRESH ORANGE SHORTCAKES

12 to 16 medium oranges
¾ cup sugar
⅓ cup butter or margarine
1 tablespoon cornstarch
¾ cup water
1½ teaspoons lemon juice
½ teaspoon grated orange rind
Shortcake Pastry
Whipped cream

Peel, section, and seed enough oranges to make 5 cups of orange sections; drain, reserving ¾ cup juice. Set aside about 1 cup of orange sections for topping.

Combine sugar, butter, orange juice, cornstarch, water, lemon juice, and orange rind in a medium saucepan. Cook over low heat, stirring constantly, until slightly thickened and bubbly. Remove from heat; stir in 4 cups orange sections.

Place 1 pastry round on each serving dish; cover each with ⅓ cup orange sauce. Top with remaining pastry rounds. Spoon remaining orange sauce over each. Garnish with a dollop of whipped cream and an orange section. Yield: ten 2½-inch servings.

Shortcake Pastry:

3 cups all-purpose flour
1 tablespoon sugar
2 teaspoons salt
1 cup vegetable oil
¼ cup milk

Combine dry ingredients; add oil and milk, stirring until mixture forms a ball.

Roll dough out on a lightly floured surface to ⅛-inch thickness; cut into rounds with a 2½-inch biscuit cutter. Using a metal spatula, carefully lift rounds and place on a lightly greased baking sheet.

Bake at 350° for 18 to 20 minutes or until rounds are lightly browned. (Pastry will be very fragile.) Cool on wire racks. Store in an airtight container, or freeze until needed. Yield: 20 pastry rounds.

Label from an early can of peaches

INDIVIDUAL PEACH SHORTCAKES

3 fresh peaches, peeled and sliced (about 2 cups)
¼ cup sugar
2 cups all-purpose flour
3 tablespoons sugar
2 teaspoons baking powder
¾ teaspoon salt
½ cup shortening
⅔ cup milk
½ cup whipping cream, whipped

Combine sliced fresh peaches and ¼ cup sugar; stir gently, and chill.

Combine flour, sugar, baking powder, and salt in a large mixing bowl; cut in shortening with pastry blender until mixture resembles coarse meal. Add milk to flour mixture; stir with a fork until a soft dough forms.

Roll dough out on a lightly floured surface to ½-inch thickness; cut out with a 3-inch cookie cutter. Carefully place rounds on an ungreased cookie sheet. Bake at 450° for 8 to 10 minutes or until lightly browned. Cool the rounds on wire racks.

Split each shortcake in half. Cover bottom of each half with ¼ cup sliced peaches, and top with a dollop of whipped cream. Replace top of each shortcake, and repeat procedure using remaining sliced peaches and whipped cream. Yield: eight 3-inch shortcakes.

FROM THE VEGETABLE GARDEN

These exhibits were part of the agricultural display at the 1915 Alabama State Fair in Birmingham.

FIESTA BEAN CAKE

½ cup butter or margarine, softened
2 cups sugar
4 eggs
4 cups cooked pinto beans, drained and mashed
2 cups all-purpose flour, divided
2 teaspoons baking soda
1 teaspoon salt
2 teaspoons ground cinnamon
1 teaspoon ground allspice
1 teaspoon ground cloves
⅛ teaspoon nutmeg

1 tablespoon plus 1 teaspoon vanilla extract
4 cups peeled, diced cooking apples
2 cups chopped pecans or walnuts
2 cups raisins
Sifted powdered sugar

Cream butter; gradually add sugar, beating well. Add eggs, one at a time, beating well after each addition. Add pinto beans, beating well. Combine 1½ cups flour, soda, salt, and spices; gradually add to bean mixture, beating well. Stir in vanilla.

Combine apples, pecans, and raisins; dredge in remaining ½ cup flour, and gently fold into batter.

Spoon batter into a greased and floured 10-inch Bundt pan. Bake at 375° for 50 to 55 minutes or until cake tests done. Cool in pan 10 minutes; remove from pan, and let cool completely. Sprinkle top of cake with powdered sugar. Yield: one 10-inch cake.

TRADITIONAL CARROT CAKE

2 cups all-purpose flour
2 teaspoons baking powder
2 teaspoons ground cinnamon
1 teaspoon salt
4 eggs
1¼ cups vegetable oil
2 cups sugar
3 cups grated carrots
Fluffy White Frosting

Combine flour, baking powder, cinnamon, and salt; set mixture aside.

Combine eggs, oil, and sugar; beat until smooth. Stir in flour mixture and carrots. Pour batter into 2 greased and floured 9-inch round cakepans.

Bake at 350° for 40 to 45 minutes or until a wooden pick inserted in center comes out clean. Cool in pans 10 minutes; remove from pans, and let cool completely.

Spread Fluffy White Frosting between layers and on top and sides of cake. Cake may be stored in refrigerator. Yield: one 2-layer cake.

Fluffy White Frosting:

1 cup sugar
½ cup light corn syrup
¼ cup water
2 egg whites
1 teaspoon vanilla extract

Combine sugar, corn syrup, and ¼ cup water in a heavy saucepan. Cook over medium heat, stirring frequently, until mixture comes to a boil and sugar is dissolved. Continue cooking, stirring frequently, until the mixture reaches soft ball stage (240°).

Beat egg whites (at room temperature) until foamy. Slowly pour hot syrup in a thin stream over egg whites while beating at medium speed of electric mixer. Turn mixer to high speed, and continue beating until stiff peaks form and frosting is thick enough to spread. Add vanilla; beat until blended. Spread immediately on cooled cake. Yield: enough for one 2-layer cake.

COTTONWOOD CARROT CAKE

2 cups sifted cake flour
2 teaspoons baking soda
½ teaspoon salt
2 teaspoons ground cinnamon
2 teaspoons ground allspice
1⅓ cups vegetable oil
4 eggs, well beaten
2 cups sugar
3 cups grated carrots
Frosting (recipe follows)

Combine flour, soda, salt, and spices; set aside.

Combine oil, eggs, and sugar; beat well. Add dry ingredients; beat well. Stir in carrots.

Pour batter into a greased and floured 13- x 9- x 2-inch baking pan. Bake at 325° for 55 minutes or until a wooden pick inserted in center comes out clean. Cool completely, and spread frosting over top of cake. Yield: one 13- x 9-inch cake.

Frosting:

1 (8-ounce) package cream cheese, softened
½ cup butter or margarine, softened
1 (16-ounce) package powdered sugar, sifted
½ cup raisins, chopped
½ cup flaked coconut
½ cup chopped pecans
1 teaspoon vanilla extract

Combine cream cheese and butter; beat until light and fluffy. Gradually add powdered sugar, beating well. Stir in remaining ingredients, beating until spreading consistency. Yield: enough for one 13- x 9-inch cake.

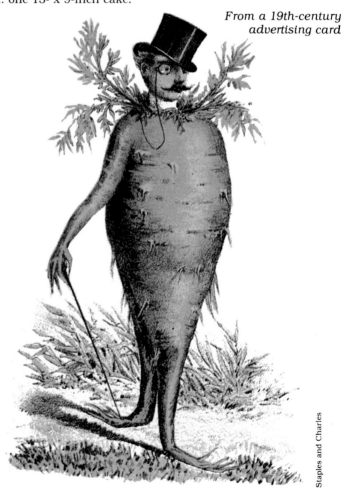

From a 19th-century advertising card

Staples and Charles

Sweet Potato Pound Cake

SWEET POTATO POUND CAKE

1 cup butter or margarine,
  softened
2 cups sugar
4 eggs
2½ cups cooked, mashed
  sweet potatoes
3 cups all-purpose flour
2 teaspoons baking powder
1 teaspoon baking soda
1 teaspoon ground
  cinnamon
½ teaspoon ground nutmeg
¼ teaspoon salt
1 teaspoon vanilla extract
½ cup flaked coconut
½ cup chopped pecans

Cream butter; gradually add sugar, beating well. Add eggs, one at a time, beating well after each addition. Add sweet potatoes; beat well.

Combine flour, baking powder, soda, cinnamon, nutmeg, and salt; gradually add to sweet potato mixture, beating well after each addition (batter will be stiff). Stir in vanilla, coconut, and pecans.

Spoon batter into a well-greased 10-inch tube pan. Bake at 350° for 1 hour and 15 minutes or until cake tests done. Cool in pan 15 minutes; remove from pan, and let cool completely. Yield: one 10-inch cake.

Note: Sweet Potato Pound Cake may be glazed or frosted with any lemon- or orange-flavored topping.

SWEET POTATO CAKE

½ cup butter or margarine,
  softened
1 cup sugar
2 eggs
1 cup cooked, mashed
  sweet potatoes
2 cups all-purpose flour
2 teaspoons baking powder
¼ teaspoon baking soda
½ teaspoon salt
½ teaspoon ground
  cinnamon
½ teaspoon ground nutmeg
¼ teaspoon ground cloves
½ cup milk
½ cup chopped pecans
Brown Sugar Caramel Icing

Cream butter; gradually add sugar, beating well. Add eggs, one at a time, beating well after each addition. Add sweet potatoes; beat well.

Combine flour, baking powder, soda, salt, and spices; add to creamed mixture alternately with milk, beginning and ending with flour mixture. Beat well after each addition. Stir in chopped pecans.

Spoon batter into a greased 9-inch square pan. Bake at 350° for 40 minutes or until a wooden pick inserted in center comes out clean. Cool. Spread Brown Sugar Caramel Icing over cake. Cut into squares to serve. Yield: one 9-inch cake.

Brown Sugar Caramel Icing:

1 cup firmly packed brown
  sugar
1 cup half-and-half
½ cup sugar
1 tablespoon butter or
  margarine
1 teaspoon vanilla extract

Combine first 3 ingredients in a heavy saucepan. Cook over medium heat, stirring frequently, until mixture comes to a boil and sugar is dissolved. Continue cooking, stirring frequently, until mixture reaches soft ball stage (240°).

Let cool slightly; add butter and vanilla, and beat until spreading consistency. Yield: enough for one 9-inch cake.

MASHED POTATO CAKE

1 cup butter or margarine,
  softened
2 cups firmly packed brown
  sugar
4 eggs
½ cup mashed potatoes
2 cups all-purpose flour
2 teaspoons baking powder
1 teaspoon ground cinnamon
1 teaspoon ground nutmeg
½ teaspoon ground cloves
1 cup milk
1 (1-ounce) square semisweet
  chocolate, melted
1 cup chopped pecans

Cream butter; gradually add brown sugar, beating well. Add eggs, one at a time, beating well after each addition. Add mashed potatoes, beating mixture well.

Combine flour, baking powder, and spices; add to creamed mixture alternately with milk, beginning and ending with flour mixture. Stir in melted chocolate and pecans.

Pour batter into a well-greased 10-inch Bundt pan. Bake at 350° for 1 hour or until cake tests done. Cool in pan 20 minutes; remove cake from pan, and cool completely before serving. Yield: one 10-inch cake.

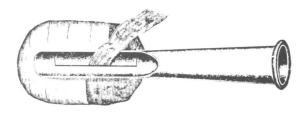

PUMPKIN CAKE

½ cup butter or margarine,
  softened
1 cup firmly packed brown
  sugar
½ cup sugar
1 egg
¾ cup cooked, mashed
  pumpkin
¼ teaspoon baking soda
⅓ cup buttermilk
2 cups all-purpose flour,
  divided
1 tablespoon baking powder
1 teaspoon salt
1 teaspoon ground
  cinnamon
⅔ cup chopped pecans
Spiced Whipped Cream
1 whole nutmeg, grated
  (optional)

Combine butter and sugar, beating well. Add egg and pumpkin; beat well.

Dissolve soda in buttermilk; stir well. Combine 1¾ cups flour, baking powder, salt, and cinnamon; add to creamed mixture alternately with buttermilk mixture, beginning and ending with flour mixture. Dredge pecans in remaining ¼ cup flour, and fold into batter.

Pour batter into 2 well-greased 8-inch round cakepans. Bake at 350° for 30 to 35 minutes or until a wooden pick inserted in center comes out clean. Cool in pans 10 minutes; remove from pans, and cool completely. Spread Spiced Whipped Cream between layers and on top of cake. Sprinkle nutmeg over top of cake, if desired. Yield: one 2-layer cake.

Spiced Whipped Cream:

1 cup whipping cream
3 tablespoons sifted
  powdered sugar
¼ teaspoon ground cinnamon
¼ teaspoon ground ginger

Beat whipping cream until foamy; gradually add powdered sugar and spices, beating until stiff peaks form. Yield: enough for one 2-layer cake.

Photographer: Mac Jamieson

GRANDMOTHER'S FAVORITES

Grandmother had her own personal favorite cakes, or was her choice sometimes limited to the ingredients she happened to have in stock? Apples or raisins, beer or whiskey, and salt pork were usually available staples. Spices were on the shelf at all times: nutmeg, ginger, mace, cinnamon, allspice, and the like. But of all the spices in the cupboard, she probably liked ginger best.

She kept not only powdered ginger for her baking, but also candied chunks for her first aid kit. A piece of ginger laid on an aching tooth, ginger tea to stimulate the innards . . . she knew all that. Her kitchen smelled of ginger and molasses. And that aroma meant gingerbread.

Every housekeeper had a certain recipe she could turn out at a moment's notice. And, although not every cook was frank enough to call that recipe a "Funeral Cake," some did. It was to be baked in the caring tradition we still observe, taking food to the home of a bereaved family.

"Stellar's Funeral Cakes" were well known in the small town of Bremond, Texas, the home of Mrs. Estelle Holland. As soon as "the news" came to her ears, Mrs. Holland would instruct her housekeeper, Stellar, to make her "Funeral Cakes" to take over to the friend's house. It was Stellar's own recipe, easy and delicious with or without icing.

It is not surprising to find Beer Cakes among our older recipes. English settlers brought along their taste for beer; it was a part of their tradition. A brewery was drawn into the original plan for William and Mary College, established in 1693. But commercial brewing had a slow start because hops and barley did not grow well in the South. There was a little commercial brewing in Virginia by the late 1700s, but beer in any quantity had to be imported from the North or from England for years to come. Interestingly, Galveston, Texas, built a brewery in 1896 as a civic enterprise, and Seawall Bond beer was a source of community pride.

We also have, bless us, Whiskey Cake. Whiskey making was not fraught with the drawbacks that hampered the brewing industry. Their intuition informed canny Southerners that corn was good for more than cornbread. One cake recipe starts like this: "Take the whiskey out of the cupboard and have a small snort for medicinal purposes. . . ."

Back to front: Prunella Cake (page 69), fruited and spiced, is topped with creamy frosting. Confederate Soldiers (page 65), twice-baked cakes, are good for a year if stored in tins. Hootenholler Whiskey Cake (page 62), no medicinal taste, but is good for what ails you.

PRESERVING THE PAST

SHORT'NIN' BREAD

2 cups all-purpose flour
½ teaspoon ground cinnamon
¼ teaspoon ground nutmeg
1½ teaspoons baking soda
½ cup buttermilk
¼ cup plus 2 tablespoons
   butter or margarine
1 cup molasses
1 egg, slightly beaten

Combine flour, cinnamon, and nutmeg in a large bowl. Mix well, and set aside. Dissolve soda in buttermilk; stir well, and set aside.

Combine butter and molasses in a heavy saucepan; bring to a boil, stirring constantly. Add to flour mixture. Stir in buttermilk mixture and egg.

Pour batter into a greased and floured 10-inch cast-iron skillet. Bake at 350° for 25 to 30 minutes or until a wooden pick inserted in center comes out clean. Cool in skillet 10 minutes; invert cake onto plate. Yield: one 10-inch cake.

Short'nin' Bread is gingerbread made without the ginger and flavored by cinnamon, nutmeg, and molasses. A well-seasoned skillet bakes it best.

STELLAR'S FUNERAL CAKES

1½ cups sugar
1½ cups all-purpose flour
1 tablespoon baking
   powder
2 eggs, beaten
1 cup milk
¼ cup shortening, melted
1 teaspoon vanilla extract
Sifted powdered sugar

Combine sugar, flour, and baking powder. Add eggs, milk, and melted shortening to dry ingredients; stir just until moistened. Stir in vanilla. Fill greased and floured muffin pans half full. Bake at 400° for 15 minutes. Remove cakes from pan, and sprinkle with powdered sugar. Yield: 2 dozen.

BEER CAKES

2 cups beer
1 cup shortening
1 cup firmly packed light
  brown sugar
1 cup firmly packed dark
  brown sugar
2 eggs
3 cups all-purpose flour,
  divided
2 teaspoons baking powder
1 teaspoon baking soda
½ teaspoon salt
2 teaspoons ground
  cinnamon
2 teaspoons ground allspice
2 teaspoons ground cloves
1 cup chopped pecans
1 cup raisins

Pour beer into a small bowl; let stand, uncovered, at room temperature overnight.

Cream shortening; gradually add sugar, beating well. Add eggs, one at a time, beating well after each addition.

Combine 2½ cups flour, baking powder, soda, salt, and spices; add to creamed mixture alternately with beer, beginning and ending with the flour mixture. Mix well after each addition.

Dredge pecans and raisins in remaining ½ cup flour; stir to coat well. Stir into batter.

Pour batter into 2 greased 9- x 5- x 3-inch loafpans. Bake at 325° for 30 minutes. Increase temperature to 350° and bake an additional 25 minutes or until a wooden pick inserted in center comes out clean. Yield: two 9-inch loaves.

SCRIPTURE CAKE

1 cup butter or margarine,
  softened
2 cups sugar
1 tablespoon honey
6 eggs
3½ cups all-purpose flour,
  divided
2 teaspoons baking
  powder
½ teaspoon salt
½ teaspoon ground cinnamon
¼ teaspoon ground cloves
⅛ teaspoon ground ginger
1 cup water
2 cups raisins
2 cups figs, chopped
1 cup chopped almonds

Cream butter in a large mixing bowl; gradually add sugar, beating well. Add honey; beat well. Add eggs, one at a time, beating well after each addition.

Combine 3 cups flour, baking powder, salt, and spices; add to creamed mixture alternately with water, beginning and ending with flour mixture. Beat well after each addition.

Dredge raisins, figs, and almonds in remaining ½ cup flour, coating well. Gently stir into batter.

Spoon batter into a greased and floured 9- x 5- x 3-inch loafpan. Bake at 325° for 1 hour and 30 minutes or until wooden pick inserted in center comes out clean. Cool in pan 10 minutes; remove cake to wire rack, and cool completely. Yield: one 9-inch loaf.

SCRIPTURE CAKE
(Original Biblical References)

Judges 5:25 He asked water, and she gave him milk; she brought forth butter in a lordly dish.

Jeremiah 6:20 To what purpose cometh there to me incense from Sheba, and the sweet cane from a far country?

Exodus 16:31 And the house of Israel called the name thereof Manna: and it was like coriander seed white; and the taste of it was like wafers made with honey.

Isaiah 10:14 And my hand hath found as a nest the riches of the people: and as one gathereth eggs that are left, have I gathered all the earth.

I Kings 4:22 And Solomon's provision for one day was thirty measures of fine flour, and threescore measures of meal.

I Corinthians 5:6 Your glorying is not good. Know ye not that a little leaven leaveneth the whole lump?

Leviticus 2:13 And every oblation of thy meat offering shalt thou season with salt.

I Kings 10:10 There came no more such abundance of spices as these which the queen of Sheba gave to King Solomon.

Exodus 17:6 Behold, I will stand before thee there upon the rock in Horeb; and thou shalt smite the rock, and there shall come water out of it, that the people may drink.

I Samuel 30:12 And they gave him a piece of a cake of figs, and two clusters of raisins.

Genesis 43:11 And their father Israel said unto them, If it must be so now, do this; take of the best fruits in the land in your vessels, and carry down the man a present, a little balm and honey, spices, and myrrh, nuts and almonds.

Some Southern distilling was done informally with the product bearing no government stamp. Some say this gave employment to the revenue agents.

HOOTENHOLLER WHISKEY CAKE

½ cup butter or margarine, softened
1 cup sugar
3 eggs
1 cup all-purpose flour
½ teaspoon baking powder
¼ teaspoon salt
½ teaspoon ground nutmeg
¼ cup milk
¼ cup molasses
¼ teaspoon baking soda
¼ cup bourbon whiskey
2 cups raisins
2 cups chopped pecans

Cream butter; gradually add sugar, beating well. Add eggs, one at a time, beating well after each addition.

Combine next 4 ingredients; add to creamed mixture alternately with milk, beginning and ending with dry ingredients. Combine molasses and baking soda; add to creamed mixture. Stir in remaining ingredients.

Pour batter into a greased and floured 9- x 5- x 3-inch loafpan. Bake at 300° for 1 hour and 40 minutes or until a wooden pick inserted in center comes out clean. Refrigerate cake for easier slicing. Yield: one 9-inch loaf.

WELCOME CAKE

½ cup butter or margarine, softened
1½ cups sugar
3 eggs
3 cups all-purpose flour, divided
1 teaspoon cream of tartar
½ teaspoon baking soda
1 cup milk
1 cup raisins
1 cup currants

Cream butter; gradually add sugar, beating well. Add eggs, one at a time, beating well after each addition. Combine 2½ cups flour, cream of tartar, and soda; add to creamed mixture alternately with milk, beginning and ending with flour mixture. Dredge fruit in remaining flour; stir into batter.

Pour batter into a well-greased 10-inch tube pan. Bake at 375° for 55 to 60 minutes or until cake tests done. Cool in pan 10 minutes; remove from pan, and let cool completely on a wire rack. Yield: one 10-inch cake.

WILLIAMSBURG PORK CAKE

½ cup brandy
2½ cups raisins
1½ cups currants
½ pound finely ground salt pork fat
1 cup boiling water
1 cup molasses
½ cup firmly packed brown sugar
3½ cups all-purpose flour
1 teaspoon baking soda
1 tablespoon ground allspice
1 tablespoon ground cinnamon
½ teaspoon ground nutmeg
½ teaspoon ground cloves

Combine brandy, raisins, and currants in a medium saucepan, stirring well; bring to a boil. Reduce heat; cook, stirring frequently, until all of the liquid is absorbed. Set aside.

Combine pork, boiling water, molasses, and sugar, beating well. Combine flour, soda, and spices; gradually add to pork mixture, stirring well. Fold in brandy-fruit mixture.

Spoon batter into a greased and floured 10-inch tube pan. Bake at 275° for 1 hour and 30 minutes or until cake tests done. Cool in pan 10 to 15 minutes; remove cake from pan, and let cool completely. Yield: one 10-inch cake.

Note: The salt pork may be soaked in water overnight and dried thoroughly before grinding. For easier grinding, meat may be cubed, partially frozen, and ground with metal blade in food processor.

PORK CAKE
(Old Recipe, Highland Springs, Va.)

Cut fine one Pound of salt Pork and pour over it two Cups of boiling Water. Add two Cups of Molaffes, one Cup of brown Sugar. Sift together feven Cups of Flour, two Tablefpoons each of Cinnamon and Allfpice, two Teafpoons each of Cloves, Nutmeg, and Soda, and beat well into the Batter. Add one Pound of well cleaned Currants and one and one half Pounds of Raifins (which have foaked overnight in one Cup of Brandy if you choofe). Bake in three large Loaf-pans in a very flow Oven about one Hour.

The Williamsburg Art of Cookery, published by Colonial Williamsburg Foundation

FROM THE CUPBOARD

BROWNSTONE FRONT CAKE

1 cup sugar
1 cup milk
2 egg yolks
¼ cup cocoa
1 cup butter or margarine, softened
2 cups sugar
3 eggs
4½ cups all-purpose flour
2 teaspoons baking soda
1 cup milk
1 teaspoon vanilla extract
Fluffy Filling

Combine 1 cup sugar, 1 cup milk, egg yolks, and cocoa in a saucepan; bring to a boil, stirring constantly until thickened. Remove from heat; cool.

Cream butter; gradually add 2 cups sugar, beating well. Add eggs, one at a time, beating well after each addition.

Combine flour and soda; add to creamed mixture alternately with 1 cup milk, beginning and ending with flour mixture. Mix well after each addition. Stir in cocoa mixture and vanilla.

Pour batter into 3 greased and floured 9-inch round cakepans. Bake at 350° for 50 minutes or until a wooden pick inserted in center comes out clean. Let cool in pans 10 minutes; remove layers from pans, and let cool completely.

Spread Fluffy Filling between layers and on top of cake. Yield: one 3-layer cake.

Fluffy Filling:

1½ cups whipping cream
3 tablespoons sifted powdered sugar
1 tablespoon plus 1½ teaspoons cocoa

Beat whipping cream until foamy. Combine sugar and cocoa; gradually add to cream, beating mixture until stiff peaks form. Yield: enough for one 3-layer cake.

Recipe for Brownstone Front Cake is from the 1895 Cotton States and International Exposition, Atlanta. Grandma's Chew Bread recipe is over 100 years old.

GRANDMA'S CHEW BREAD

1 (16-ounce) package light brown sugar
4 eggs
2 cups all-purpose flour
½ teaspoon salt
1 teaspoon vanilla extract
1 cup chopped pecans

Combine sugar and eggs in a heavy saucepan, stirring well; cook over medium heat, stirring constantly, until sugar dissolves. Remove from heat. Add remaining ingredients, stirring mixture well.

Spoon mixture into a greased and floured 15- x 10- x 1-inch jellyroll pan. Bake at 400° for 15 minutes or until golden brown. Cool, and cut into squares. Yield: about 3 dozen.

HONEY-CRISP
COFFEE CAKE

3 tablespoons shortening
½ cup sugar
1 egg
1½ cups all-purpose flour
2 teaspoons baking powder
½ teaspoon salt
½ cup milk
Honey-Crisp Topping

Cream shortening and sugar; add egg, beating well.

Combine flour, baking powder, and salt; add to creamed mixture alternately with milk, beginning and ending with flour mixture.

Pour batter into a greased 9-inch square cakepan. Spread Honey-Crisp Topping evenly over batter. Bake at 400° for 25 minutes or until a wooden pick inserted in center comes out clean. Cool in pan 10 minutes. Cut into squares to serve. Yield: one 9-inch cake.

Honey-Crisp Topping:

3 tablespoons butter or
  margarine, softened
⅓ cup honey
½ cup crushed cornflakes
½ cup drained crushed
  pineapple
¼ cup flaked coconut

Combine butter and honey, beating until light and fluffy. Gently stir in remaining ingredients. Yield: enough for one 9-inch cake.

City Hall Coffee Cake is a treat served warm with coffee.

"Early rising is also essential to the good government of a family. A late breakfast deranges the whole business of the day, and throws a portion of it on the next, which opens the door for confusion to enter."

In spite of what Mary Randolph admonished in 1831, these coffee cakes are delicious for a late breakfast—and are guaranteed not to ruin your day.

CITY HALL COFFEE CAKE

½ cup sugar
2 teaspoons ground
  cinnamon
1 cup chopped pecans
1 cup flaked coconut
½ cup butter or margarine,
  softened
1 cup sugar
2 eggs
1¾ cups all-purpose flour
1 teaspoon baking powder
1 teaspoon baking soda
½ teaspoon salt
1 (8-ounce) carton
  commercial sour cream

Combine ½ cup sugar, cinnamon, pecans, and coconut; stir well, and set aside.

Cream butter; gradually add 1 cup sugar, beating well. Add eggs; beat well.

Combine flour, baking powder, soda, and salt; add to creamed mixture alternately with sour cream, beginning and ending with flour mixture.

Spoon half of batter into a greased 10-inch tube pan; sprinkle half of pecan mixture over batter. Repeat layers. Bake at 350° for 45 to 50 minutes or until cake tests done.

Cool 5 minutes in pan; invert cake onto serving plate. Cool. Yield: one 10-inch coffee cake.

Julia Shirley's great-aunt lived between Meridian and Newton, Mississippi, during the Civil War. She made "soldier" cakes for Confederate soldiers trudging toward southern Louisiana.

CONFEDERATE SOLDIERS

6 eggs, separated
1½ cups sugar
1 cup candied citron
¾ cup chopped blanched almonds
2 cups all-purpose flour, divided

Beat egg yolks until thick and lemon colored; gradually add sugar, beating well. Dredge citron and almonds in ½ cup flour; stir into yolk mixture.

Combine egg whites (at room temperature) and remaining 1½ cups flour, beating until thick. Stir in yolk mixture.

Spoon batter into a greased 15- x 10- x 1-inch jellyroll pan. Bake at 450° for 10 minutes. Remove from oven, and cut into bars. Turn each bar on its side, and return to oven for 4 to 5 minutes. Cool thoroughly. Yield: about 4 dozen.

HOT WATER GINGERBREAD

⅓ cup shortening
⅔ cup boiling water
1 cup molasses
1 egg, beaten
2¾ cups all-purpose flour
1½ teaspoons baking soda
½ teaspoon salt
1 teaspoon ground cinnamon
1½ teaspoons ground ginger
¼ teaspoon ground cloves
Tangy Lemon Sauce

Melt shortening in boiling water; add molasses and egg. Combine the dry ingredients; add to molasses mixture. Pour batter into a greased 9-inch square pan. Bake at 350° for 30 to 35 minutes or until a wooden pick inserted in center comes out clean. Cool before cutting into squares. Top each serving with about 1 tablespoon Tangy Lemon Sauce. Yield: nine 3-inch squares.

Tangy Lemon Sauce:

1 cup sugar
1 egg, beaten
1 tablespoon grated lemon rind
Juice of 2 lemons (about 3½ tablespoons)
1 tablespoon butter or margarine, softened

Combine all ingredients, except butter, in top of double boiler. Bring water to a boil and reduce heat to low. Cook, stirring constantly, until thickened. Remove from heat and stir in butter. Cool slightly. Yield: about 1 cup.

OLD-FASHIONED GINGERBREAD

⅓ cup shortening
1 cup sugar
2 eggs
1 (8-ounce) carton commercial sour cream
½ cup molasses
2 cups all-purpose flour
1 teaspoon baking soda
½ teaspoon salt
1½ teaspoons ground ginger
¼ teaspoon ground cloves
Creamy Lemon Frosting

Cream shortening; add sugar, beating well. Add eggs, one at a time, beating well after each addition. Stir in sour cream and molasses. Combine dry ingredients; gently fold into batter.

Pour batter into a well-greased 13- x 9- x 2-inch baking pan. Bake at 350° for 35 minutes or until a wooden pick inserted in center comes out clean. Cool completely. Spread Creamy Lemon Frosting over top of cake. Cut gingerbread into squares to serve. Yield: one 13- x 9-inch cake.

Creamy Lemon Frosting:

¼ cup butter or margarine, softened
About 5½ cups sifted powdered sugar, divided
⅛ teaspoon grated lemon rind
¼ cup lemon juice
1 tablespoon whipping cream

Cream butter and 2 cups sugar until fluffy. Add lemon rind, juice, and whipping cream, beating well. Gradually add remaining sugar, beating until spreading consistency. Yield: enough for one 13- x 9-inch cake.

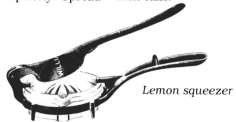

Lemon squeezer

MISSISSIPPI RIVER STAGE PLANKS

1 cup butter or margarine, softened
½ cup sugar
2 cups cane syrup
½ cup boiling water
1 tablespoon ground cinnamon
1 teaspoon ground cloves
1½ teaspoons ground ginger
½ teaspoon salt
6½ to 7 cups all-purpose flour
Sifted powdered sugar

Cream butter; gradually add ½ cup sugar, beating until light and fluffy. Add next 6 ingredients, beating until smooth.

Add flour, ½ cup at a time, beating well after each addition (dough will be stiff). Press dough into 6- x 1½-inch rectangles. Carefully transfer to ungreased cookie sheets. Bake at 300° for 15 to 20 minutes. Remove to wire racks, and sprinkle with powdered sugar. Yield: 1½ dozen.

LAZY-DAZY CAKE

2 eggs
1 cup sugar
1 cup all-purpose flour
1 teaspoon baking powder
¼ teaspoon salt
½ cup milk, scalded
1 tablespoon butter or margarine, softened
1 teaspoon vanilla extract
Topping (recipe follows)

Beat eggs; gradually add sugar, beating well. Combine flour, baking powder, and salt; add to egg mixture, beating mixture well.

Combine milk and butter, stirring to melt butter; add to flour mixture, beating well. Stir in vanilla.

Pour batter into a greased and floured 8-inch square pan. Bake at 350° for 30 minutes or until a wooden pick inserted in center comes out clean.

Immediately pour topping over cake in pan; broil 1 to 2 minutes or until lightly

The first steamboat plied the Mississippi in 1811, and the next fifty years were a romantic period in the South. Evocative of the era is the lithograph by Currier and Ives, as well as Mississippi River Stage Planks, an unusual form of New Orleans Gingerbread dating back to 1900. Butter was undoubtedly used, as the recipe predates margarine. Instead of being baked before cutting, the dough is formed into "planks," then baked as cookies.

Champions of the Mississippi *lithograph by Currier and Ives after F.F. Palmer, c.1866.*

browned. Cut into squares to serve. Yield: one 8-inch cake.

Topping:

½ cup plus 1 tablespoon firmly packed brown sugar
¼ cup plus 1 tablespoon butter or margarine, melted
¼ cup half-and-half
½ cup flaked coconut
½ cup chopped pecans

Combine all ingredients, stirring well. Yield: enough for one 8-inch cake.

ICE CREAM CAKE

¼ cup plus 2 tablespoons shortening
1 cup sugar
2 eggs
1½ cups all-purpose flour
1 teaspoon baking powder
⅛ teaspoon salt
½ cup milk
1 teaspoon vanilla extract
Vanilla ice cream (optional)
Sliced fresh strawberries (optional)

Cream shortening; gradually add sugar, beating well. Add eggs, one at a time, beating well after each addition.

Combine flour, baking powder, and salt; add to creamed mixture alternately with milk, beginning and ending with flour mixture. Beat well after each addition. Stir in vanilla.

Pour batter into a greased and floured 9- x 5- x 3-inch loafpan. Bake at 350° for 50 minutes or until a wooden pick inserted in center comes out clean. Cool in pan 10 minutes; remove from pan and cool. Slice cake and serve with ice cream and strawberries, if desired. Yield: one 9-inch loaf.

SAUERKRAUT CAKE

⅔ cup butter or margarine, softened
1½ cups sugar
3 eggs
1 teaspoon vanilla
2¼ cups all-purpose flour, divided
½ cup cocoa
1 teaspoon baking powder
1 teaspoon baking soda
¼ teaspoon salt
1 cup water
⅔ cup chopped sauerkraut, drained
⅓ cup chopped pecans
Rich Butter Frosting

Cream butter; gradually add sugar, beating well. Add eggs, one at a time, beating well after each addition. Stir in vanilla.

Combine 2 cups flour, cocoa, baking powder, soda, and salt; add to creamed mixture alternately with water, beginning and ending with dry ingredients. Mix well after each addition. Dredge sauerkraut and pecans in remaining ¼ cup flour; stir to coat well. Stir mixture into batter.

Spoon batter into an ungreased 15- x 10- x 1-inch jellyroll pan. Bake at 350° for 35 to 40 minutes or until a wooden pick inserted in center comes out clean. Cool completely. Frost with Rich Butter Frosting. Cut cake into squares to serve. Yield: one 15- x 10-inch cake.

Rich Butter Frosting:

¼ cup plus 1 tablespoon all-purpose flour
1 cup milk
1 cup butter
1 cup sugar
1 teaspoon vanilla extract

Combine flour and milk in a medium saucepan; cook over medium heat until thickened. Remove from heat; set aside.

Cream butter; gradually add sugar, beating until light and fluffy. Stir in vanilla. Add flour mixture to creamed mixture, beating until very smooth. Yield: enough for one 15- x 10-inch cake.

Making sauerkraut

A TASTE OF FRUIT

BANANA-NUT CAKE

½ cup shortening
1 cup sugar
2 eggs
2 cups mashed ripe bananas
2 cups all-purpose flour
1 teaspoon baking powder
1 teaspoon baking soda
½ teaspoon salt
1 cup chopped pecans

Cream shortening; gradually add sugar, beating well. Add eggs, one at a time, beating well after each addition. Add bananas, and mix until smooth.

Combine flour, baking powder, soda, and salt; add to creamed mixture, stirring just until moistened. Stir in chopped pecans.

Pour batter into a greased and floured 9- x 5- x 3-inch loafpan. Bake at 350° for 1 hour and 15 minutes. Cool in pan 10 minutes. Remove cake to wire rack to complete cooling. Yield: one 9-inch loaf.

ORANGE-DATE CAKE

1 cup shortening
2 cups sugar
4 eggs
1 teaspoon baking soda
1⅓ cups buttermilk
4 cups all-purpose flour, divided
1 (8-ounce) package chopped dates
1 cup chopped pecans
2 tablespoons grated orange rind
Orange Glaze

Cream shortening; gradually add sugar, beating well. Add eggs, one at a time, beating well after each addition.

Dissolve soda in buttermilk. Add 3½ cups flour to creamed mixture alternately with buttermilk mixture, beginning and ending with flour. Beat well after each addition. Dredge dates, pecans, and rind in remaining ½ cup flour.

Spoon batter into a greased 10-inch tube pan. Bake at 350° for 1 hour and 25 minutes or until cake tests done.

While cake is still warm, prick surface at 1-inch intervals with a wooden pick; pour Orange Glaze over cake in pan. Cool 10 minutes; remove from pan and cool completely. Yield: one 10-inch cake.

Orange Glaze:

2 teaspoons grated orange rind
½ cup orange juice
1 cup sugar

Combine all ingredients in a small saucepan; bring to a boil, stirring constantly, until sugar is dissolved. Yield: ½ cup.

Transferring bananas from ships to refrigerator cars and warehouses at Mobile, Alabama, c.1900.

Food chopper

PRUNELLA CAKE

⅔ cup prunes, chopped
½ cup water
½ cup shortening
1 cup sugar
2 eggs
1⅓ cups all-purpose flour, divided
1 teaspoon baking powder
1 teaspoon baking soda
½ teaspoon salt
1 teaspoon ground nutmeg
1 teaspoon ground cinnamon
1 teaspoon ground allspice
⅔ cup buttermilk
Cream Frosting
6 to 8 whole sugar-coated prunes (optional)

Combine prunes and water in a saucepan. Bring to a boil; cover and simmer 2 minutes. Drain; reserving 2 tablespoons juice for frosting. Set aside.

Cream shortening; gradually add sugar, beating well. Add eggs, one at a time, beating well after each addition.

Combine 1 cup flour and remaining dry ingredients; add to creamed mixture alternately with buttermilk, beginning and ending with flour mixture. Dredge prunes in remaining ⅓ cup flour; stir to coat well. Stir into batter.

Pour batter into 2 greased and floured 9-inch round cakepans. Bake at 350° for 30 minutes or until a wooden pick inserted in center comes out clean. Cool in pans 10 minutes; remove layers from pans, and cool completely. Spread Cream Frosting between layers and on top and sides of cake. Garnish with whole sugar-coated prunes, if desired. Yield: one 2-layer cake.

Cream Frosting:

¼ cup butter, softened
1 (16-ounce) package powdered sugar, sifted
2 tablespoons lemon juice
2 tablespoons reserved prune juice

Cream butter, beating well. Add remaining ingredients; beat until smooth. Yield: enough for one 2-layer cake.

PRUNE CAKE

1¼ cups cooked, pitted prunes, chopped
1 cup water
½ cup shortening
1 cup sugar
1 egg
1 teaspoon baking soda
½ cup buttermilk
2¼ cups all-purpose flour, divided
1 teaspoon ground cinnamon
1 teaspoon grated lemon rind
1 teaspoon vanilla extract
¾ cup chopped pecans

Combine prunes and water in a medium saucepan. Bring to a boil; cover and simmer 5 minutes. Drain and set aside.

Cream shortening; gradually add sugar, beating well. Add egg; beat well.

Dissolve soda in buttermilk. Combine 2 cups flour and cinnamon; add to creamed mixture alternately with buttermilk mixture, beginning and ending with flour mixture. Stir in prunes, lemon rind, and vanilla. Dredge pecans in remaining ¼ cup flour; stir into batter.

Pour batter into a greased and waxed paper-lined 9- x 5- x 3-inch loafpan. Bake at 350° for 1 hour and 10 minutes or until a wooden pick inserted in center comes out clean. Cool in pan 10 minutes; remove from pan. Yield: one 9-inch loaf.

RAISIN-APPLESAUCE CAKE

½ cup butter or margarine, softened
1 cup sugar
1 egg
2 cups all-purpose flour, divided
1 teaspoon baking soda
¼ teaspoon salt
1 teaspoon ground cinnamon
½ teaspoon ground nutmeg
1 cup applesauce
1 teaspoon grated lemon rind
1 cup raisins
1 cup chopped pecans

Raisin seeder

Cream butter; gradually add sugar, beating well. Add egg, mixing well.

Combine 1½ cups flour, soda, salt, cinnamon, and nutmeg; add to creamed mixture. Stir in applesauce and lemon rind. Dredge the raisins and pecans in remaining ½ cup flour; stir to coat well. Fold into batter.

Pour batter into a greased and waxed paper-lined 8-inch square pan. Bake at 350° for 1 hour or until a wooden pick inserted comes out clean. Cool. Yield: one 8-inch cake.

TENNESSEE APPLE UPSIDE-DOWN CAKE

1½ tablespoons butter or margarine
½ cup firmly packed brown sugar
1 teaspoon ground cinnamon
3 medium cooking apples, peeled, cored, and cut into rings
¼ cup shortening
¼ cup firmly packed brown sugar
½ cup molasses
1 egg
1¼ cups all-purpose flour
¾ teaspoon baking soda
¼ teaspoon salt
¾ teaspoon ground ginger
½ teaspoon ground cinnamon
½ cup buttermilk
Whipped cream (optional)

Melt butter in a 9-inch cast-iron skillet. Combine ½ cup brown sugar and 1 teaspoon cinnamon; sprinkle over butter in skillet. Arrange apple slices on sugar mixture. Set aside.

Combine shortening, ¼ cup brown sugar, and molasses, creaming well. Add egg; beat well. Combine flour, soda, salt, and spices; add to creamed mixture alternately with buttermilk, beginning and ending with flour mixture.

Pour batter evenly over apple slices in prepared skillet. Bake at 350° for 50 minutes or until cake tests done. Cool 15 minutes, and invert onto plate. Serve warm with whipped cream, if desired. Yield: one 9-inch cake.

Molasses pitcher

CHERRY UPSIDE-DOWN CAKE

½ cup firmly packed brown sugar
1 (16-ounce) can tart cherries, undrained
⅓ cup shortening
1 cup sugar
1 egg
1¾ cups all-purpose flour
1 teaspoon baking powder
½ teaspoon salt
1 cup evaporated milk
1 teaspoon vanilla extract
Cherry Sauce
Whipped cream

Grease a 13- x 9- x 2-inch baking pan; sprinkle brown sugar evenly over bottom of pan. Drain cherries, reserving juice for Cherry Sauce; add enough water to juice to equal 1½ cups. Set aside. Spoon cherries evenly over brown sugar. Set aside.

Cream shortening; gradually add sugar, beating well. Add egg, beating well. Combine flour, baking powder, and salt; add to creamed mixture alternately with milk, beginning and ending with flour mixture. Stir in vanilla.

Pour batter over cherries in pan. Bake at 350° for 40 minutes or until a wooden pick inserted in center comes out clean. Cut into squares, and spoon Cherry Sauce over top. Garnish with whipped cream. Yield: twelve 3-inch squares.

Cherry Sauce:

1½ cups reserved cherry juice
½ cup sugar
1½ tablespoons cornstarch
⅛ teaspoon almond extract
1 drop red food coloring

Combine reserved cherry juice, sugar, and cornstarch in a medium saucepan; stir well. Cook over medium heat about 20 minutes, stirring constantly, or until mixture is thickened. Remove from heat; add almond extract and red food coloring, stirring well. Cool completely. Yield: 1 cup.

Cherry pitter

PINEAPPLE UPSIDE-DOWN CAKE

½ cup butter or margarine, softened
¾ cup firmly packed brown sugar
1 (8-ounce) can sliced pineapple, drained
9 maraschino cherries
3 eggs, separated
1 cup sugar
1 cup all-purpose flour
¼ teaspoon salt
¼ cup plus 1 tablespoon water
1 teaspoon vanilla extract

Cream butter; gradually add brown sugar, beating until light and fluffy. Spread creamed mixture evenly in a 9-inch cast-iron skillet. Arrange pineapple slices and cherries evenly over creamed mixture.

Beat egg yolks until thick and lemon colored. Gradually add sugar, beating well. Combine flour and salt; add to yolk mixture alternately with water, stirring well after each addition. Stir in vanilla.

Beat egg whites (at room temperature) until stiff peaks form; fold into batter.

Spoon batter evenly over pineapple slices in skillet. Bake at 350° for 50 minutes or until wooden pick inserted in center comes out clean. Cool 30 minutes in pan, and invert cake onto serving plate. Yield: one 9-inch cake.

PINEAPPLE-AMBROSIA UPSIDE-DOWN CAKE

¼ cup butter or margarine
⅓ cup firmly packed brown
   sugar
1 (20-ounce) can sliced
   pineapple, drained
7 maraschino cherries
6 walnuts, halved
2½ tablespoons shortening
2½ tablespoons butter or
   margarine
1 teaspoon grated orange
   rind
⅔ cup sugar
1 egg
1¼ cups all-purpose flour
2 teaspoons baking powder
½ teaspoon salt
½ cup milk
⅓ cup flaked coconut
1 teaspoon vanilla extract
Whipped cream (optional)

Melt butter in a 10-inch cast-iron skillet; sprinkle brown sugar evenly over butter. Arrange 7 pineapple slices on sugar. Cut remaining pineapple slices in half; line sides of pan, keeping cut sides up. Place a cherry in the center of each whole pineapple slice; arrange walnuts between slices.

Combine shortening, butter, and orange rind; cream well. Gradually add ⅔ cup sugar, beating until light and fluffy. Add egg; beat well.

Combine flour, baking powder, and salt; add to creamed mixture alternately with milk, beginning and ending with flour mixture. Beat well after each addition. Stir in coconut and vanilla.

Spoon batter evenly over pineapple slices in prepared skillet. Bake at 350° for 45 minutes or until a wooden pick inserted in center comes out clean. Cool in skillet 10 minutes, and invert cake onto serving plate.

Serve warm with a dollop of whipped cream, if desired. Yield: one 10-inch cake.

Pineapple-Ambrosia Upside-Down Cake

Pineapple, native to Central and South America, came into ports in the Deep South even when the Spanish were still in charge there. By the middle 1700s, pineapple was regularly on the market even in New York, imported from the West Indies. There is an abundance of 18th-century recipes using grated pineapple in chutney, pudding, and such. But the first recipe for Pineapple Upside-Down Cake probably came in a booklet offered by a commercial cannery; the uniform slices had a mighty appeal to the home cook. Variations came into being in a hurry; cooks quickly realized that a simple batter poured over almost any fruit would turn bottoms up to make an attractive dessert.

AFTERNOON SURPRISES

Give the Southern baker credit for good judgment. She can be well aware that company's dropping by in the afternoon, but she doesn't spend the morning in a nervous twit. A little snack perhaps, but the emphasis is on visitation, not impressive comestibles. All she means to convey is "I'm glad you came." And it gives her a chance to utter innocent disclaimers such as "Oh this little John Garner Cake just took a minute. I like it with tea, don't you?"

Baked in a loaf like the John Garner Cake, in conventional cakepans like the Red Watermelon Cake, or in cupcakes like lots of surprises are, these are the spicy or fruited or nut-rich goodies that bring miles of smiles.

In Texas they call it Wacky Cake; in Alabama, Crazy Cake, but chocolate lovers call it wonderful. For those who love any flavor so long as it is chocolate, a section of this chapter is sacrosanct. Mississippi Mud Cake will cure the most desperate craving for chocolate. It is so dark, so moist, and so rich that one person was heard to say that he found it "indistinguishable from the mud of any other state." Never mind, you all; there is always someone who prefers vanilla.

How do we come by a recipe called Chocolate Sheath Cake? One guess is that sheath is a corruption of the word sheet. Call it what you will, only remember to serve it to hungry after-schoolers with glasses of milk. The only question on their lips will be, "Is there any more?"

Red Watermelon Cake dates back at least a century, and is in the ancient and merry tradition of making a dish look like something it is not. Marjorie Kinnan Rawlings, in her *Cross Creek Cookery*, 1942, remembered Watermelon Cake baked as a deep loaf cake. Our cake, however, is a layer cake tinted a watermelon red and laced with raisins to represent seeds. The frosting is a not-so-delicate green, producing a cake guaranteed to delight young people in any household.

In all baking, it is good to know that the oven is accurately functioning at the desired temperature. Great-great grandmother knew this, but she trembled when she read these instructions: ". . . Many test their ovens this way: if the hand can be held in from twenty to thirty-five seconds it is a 'quick' oven, from thirty-five to forty-five seconds it is a 'moderate,' and from forty-five to sixty seconds it is 'slow.'"

Clockwise from top: Mamaw's Confederate Jumbles (page 85), Gretchen's Cracker Cake (page 75), Chocolate Sheath Cake (page 81), and Marble Molasses Cake (page 77). Any one of these makes a "stop by for coffee" into a memorable visit.

VERY SPECIAL SNACKS

The pleasure of anticipation as a cake is covered with drifts of snow-white coconut. Mother passes along a tradition.

TOASTED COCONUT CAKE

½ cup butter or margarine,
  softened
2 cups sugar
4 eggs, separated
2½ cups all-purpose flour
1 tablespoon baking powder
½ teaspoon salt
1 cup milk
1 teaspoon vanilla extract
Toasted Coconut Topping

Cream butter; gradually add sugar, beating well. Beat egg yolks, and add to creamed mixture; beat well.

Combine flour, baking powder, and salt; add to creamed mixture alternately with milk, beginning and ending with flour mixture. Stir in vanilla.

Beat the egg whites (at room

temperature) until stiff peaks form; fold into batter. Pour batter into greased and floured 13- x 9- x 2-inch baking pan. Bake at 350° for 50 minutes or until a wooden pick inserted in center comes out clean. Spread Toasted Coconut Topping evenly over cake. Broil 2 to 3 minutes or until golden brown. Cool, and cut into squares. Yield: one 13- x 9-inch cake.

Toasted Coconut Topping:

¼ cup butter or margarine,
  softened
1 cup firmly packed brown
  sugar
¾ cup half-and-half
2 cups flaked coconut

Combine all ingredients; mix well. Yield: enough for one 13- x 9-inch cake.

HASTY CAKE

⅓ cup butter or margarine,
  softened
1 cup sugar
1 egg
1¾ cups all-purpose flour
1 tablespoon baking powder
¼ teaspoon salt
⅔ cup milk
1 teaspoon vanilla extract
Quick 'n Easy Frosting

Cream butter in a large mixing bowl; gradually add sugar, beating well. Add egg, beating mixture well.

Combine dry ingredients; add to creamed mixture alternately with milk, beginning and ending with flour mixture. Stir in vanilla.

Pour batter into a greased and floured 8-inch square pan. Bake at 350° for 25 to 30 minutes or until a wooden pick inserted in center comes out clean. Cool in pan 10 minutes; remove from pan, and let cool completely. Spread Quick 'n Easy Frosting on top and sides of cake. Yield: one 8-inch cake.

Quick 'n Easy Frosting:

½ cup butter or margarine,
  softened
1 egg white
2½ cups sifted powdered
  sugar
1 teaspoon vanilla extract

Combine butter and egg white (at room temperature); beat well. Gradually add powdered sugar, beating mixture well after each addition. Gently stir in vanilla. Yield: enough for one 8-inch cake.

GRETCHEN'S CRACKER CAKE

½ cup butter, softened
2 cups sugar
4 eggs
1 cup all-purpose flour
1 cup cracker crumbs
1½ teaspoons baking powder
1 cup milk
1 teaspoon lemon extract
1 cup chopped pecans
Lemon Glaze
Lemon slices

Cream butter; gradually add sugar, beating well. Add eggs, one at a time, beating well after each addition.

Combine flour, cracker crumbs, and baking powder; add to creamed mixture alternately with milk, beginning and ending with flour mixture. Mix well after each addition. Stir in lemon extract and chopped pecans.

Pour batter into 2 greased and floured 8-inch round cakepans. Bake at 350° for 25 minutes or until a wooden pick inserted in center comes out clean. Cool in pans 10 minutes; remove layers from pans, and let cool completely. Spoon Lemon Glaze between layers and over top of cake. Garnish with lemon slices. Yield: one 2-layer cake.

Lemon Glaze:

1 cup sugar
1 tablespoon cornstarch
1 teaspoon butter or margarine
1 cup boiling water
1 egg yolk
1 teaspoon lemon juice

Combine sugar, cornstarch, and butter in a heavy saucepan; mix well. Stir in boiling water; cook over low heat, stirring constantly, until thickened.

Combine egg yolk and lemon juice; stir well. Gradually stir about one-fourth of hot mixture into yolk; add yolk mixture to remaining hot mixture, stirring constantly. Continue to cook until thickened. Chill glaze thoroughly before using. Yield: about 1 cup.

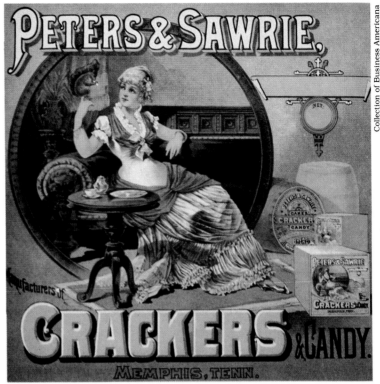

Label from a Memphis, Tennessee firm

EGGS ON TOAST

1 (10-inch) pound cake, cut into 1-inch slices
1 cup whipping cream
2 tablespoons sugar
2 (17-ounce) cans apricot halves, well drained

Lightly toast pound cake slices; set aside.

Beat whipping cream until foamy; gradually add sugar, beating until soft peaks form.

Spoon a dollop (about 2 tablespoons) of whipped cream on each toasted cake slice. Place 1 apricot half, cut side down, in center of whipped cream. Serve immediately Yield: about 20 servings.

Some of the recipes in this section could rightly be called "neo-heritage" if one reflects on the short history of some of the ingredients. Fruit cocktail in cans, for instance, or ready-to-use coconut. Vegetable shortening harkens back only to 1880. That handy bottle of vanilla? Before Thomas Jefferson introduced it from France in 1791, cooks flavored their cakes with rose water, orange flower water, caraway seed, and ambergris ("ambergrease").

Powdered sugar? As late as 1700, sugar reached the kitchen in the form of a 9- or 10-pound cone, and rock-hard. It was up to the cook to break it up, then pound it, and sift it. It was this sifted sugar old recipes meant by "powdered"; it was comparable to today's granulated sugar.

FRUIT COCKTAIL CAKE

2 cups sugar
2 cups all-purpose flour
1 teaspoon baking soda
½ teaspoon salt
1 (17-ounce) can fruit
  cocktail, undrained
Topping (recipe follows)

Combine dry ingredients in a medium mixing bowl; mix well. Stir in fruit cocktail. Pour batter into a greased and floured 13- x 9- x 2-inch baking pan. Bake at 350° for 55 to 60 minutes or until a wooden pick inserted in center comes out clean.

Remove from oven and immediately spoon the topping over cake. Cool completely. Cut into squares to serve. Yield: one 13- x 9-inch cake.

Topping:

1 (5.33-ounce) can evaporated
  milk
1 cup sugar
½ cup butter or margarine
½ cup chopped pecans

Combine milk, sugar, and butter in a medium saucepan; mix well. Cook over medium heat, stirring constantly, about 10 minutes or until mixture is thickened. Remove from heat, and stir in chopped pecans. Yield: enough for one 13- x 9-inch cake.

JOHN GARNER CAKE

2 cups water
2½ cups raisins
½ cup shortening
2 cups sugar
2 teaspoons ground
  cinnamon
½ teaspoon ground cloves
2 teaspoons baking soda
½ cup hot water
3¾ cups all-purpose flour
⅛ teaspoon salt

Place 2 cups water in a large saucepan; bring to a boil. Add raisins, shortening, sugar, cinnamon, and cloves. Cook 10 minutes; remove mixture from heat, and cool.

Dissolve soda in ½ cup hot water; add to raisin mixture. Add flour and salt; mix well.

Spoon batter into 2 greased 8½- x 4½- x 3-inch loafpans. Bake at 350° for 1 hour and 10 minutes or until a wooden pick inserted in center comes out clean. Cool in pan 10 minutes; invert onto serving platter. Yield: 2 loaves.

John Nance Garner was born in Red River County, Texas, in 1869. After some irregular schooling, he "read law" in a small town office and was admitted to the bar in 1890. After serving two terms in the Texas legislature, he was sent to Congress, where he served from 1903 until 1933. At that point, he became Vice President under Franklin D. Roosevelt. His years in Washington never caused him to forget his love for Texas and the rural life. He is one of many famous people for whom Southerners have named some of their cakes. President James K. Polk, a North Carolinian, and General Robert E. Lee of Virginia are in that number.

John Nance Garner, in 1936, feeding chickens

Pineapple Meringue Cake: Coconut meringue baked as filling along with the layers

PINEAPPLE MERINGUE CAKE

½ cup butter or margarine,
  softened
1 cup sugar
4 eggs, separated
2 cups all-purpose flour
¾ cup milk
¾ cup sugar
1 cup flaked coconut
1 cup whipping cream
½ cup sugar
1 (8-ounce) can crushed
  pineapple, well drained

Cream butter; gradually add 1 cup sugar, beating well. Add egg yolks; beat well. Add flour to creamed mixture alternately with milk, beginning and ending with flour. Pour batter into 2 greased and floured 8-inch round cakepans; set aside.

Beat egg whites (at room temperature) until foamy. Gradually add ¾ cup sugar, one tablespoon at a time, beating until stiff peaks form. Add coconut; stir well. Spread meringue mixture over cake batter, sealing to edge of cakepan. Bake at 325° for 30 to 35 minutes or until meringue is lightly browned. Cool in pans 10 minutes; gently remove layers from pans, and let cool completely.

Place first layer on serving plate, meringue side up. Place second layer on top of first, meringue side down.

Beat whipping cream until foamy; gradually add ½ cup sugar, beating until stiff peaks form. Fold in pineapple. Spread whipped cream over top of cake and around lower edge of cake. Yield: one 2-layer cake.

MARBLE MOLASSES CAKE

½ cup butter or margarine,
  softened
1 cup sugar
2 eggs
2 cups sifted cake flour
2 teaspoons baking powder
¼ teaspoon salt
⅔ cup milk
¼ teaspoon ground ginger
1 teaspoon ground cinnamon
½ teaspoon ground cloves
3 tablespoons molasses

Cream butter; gradually add sugar, beating well. Add eggs, one at a time, beating mixture well after each addition.

Combine flour, baking powder, and salt; add to creamed mixture alternately with milk, beginning and ending with flour mixture.

Divide batter in half; add remaining ingredients to one half of batter, stirring until smooth. Drop batter by tablespoonfuls into a greased 9- x 5- x 3-inch loafpan, alternating dark and light mixtures. Bake at 350° for 1 hour or until a wooden pick inserted in center comes out clean. Yield: 1 loaf.

PRALINE CAKE

¼ cup shortening
¾ cup sugar
1 egg
1½ cups sifted cake flour
1½ teaspoons baking powder
¼ teaspoon salt
⅔ cup milk
1 teaspoon vanilla extract
Praline Glaze

Cream shortening and sugar; add egg, beating well. Combine flour, baking powder, and salt; add to creamed mixture alternately with milk, beginning and ending with flour mixture. Stir in vanilla.

Pour batter into a heavily greased 8-inch round or square cakepan. Bake at 350° for 25 to 30 minutes or until a wooden pick inserted in center comes out clean. Cool slightly. Spread Praline Glaze over cake. Bake at 350° for 5 minutes. Yield: one 8-inch cake.

Praline Glaze:

1 tablespoon plus 1 teaspoon all-purpose flour
½ cup firmly packed brown sugar
¼ cup butter or margarine, melted
2 tablespoons water
¾ cup chopped pecans

Combine first 4 ingredients, mixing well. Stir in chopped pecans. Yield: enough for one 8-inch cake.

QUICK CAKE

½ cup shortening
1 cup sugar
2 eggs, separated
2 cups all-purpose flour
2 teaspoons baking powder
1 cup milk
Quick Fudge Frosting

Cream shortening; gradually add sugar, beating well. Add egg yolks; beat well.

Combine flour and baking powder; add to creamed mixture alternately with milk, beginning and ending with flour mixture.

Beat egg whites (at room temperature) until soft peaks form; gently fold into batter.

Pour batter into a lightly greased and floured 13- x 9- x 2-inch baking pan. Bake at 350° for 30 minutes or until a wooden pick inserted in center comes out clean. Cool in pan 10 minutes. Spread Quick Fudge Frosting on top of warm cake. Cut cake into squares to serve. Yield: one 13- x 9-inch cake.

Quick Fudge Frosting:

1 cup firmly packed brown sugar
3 tablespoons cocoa
3 tablespoons shortening
1 tablespoon butter or margarine
¼ teaspoon salt
About ⅓ cup milk
1½ cups sifted powdered sugar
1 teaspoon vanilla extract

Combine brown sugar, cocoa, shortening, butter, salt, and milk in a medium saucepan. Cook over medium heat, stirring frequently, until mixture comes to a boil. Cook 3 minutes, stirring constantly. Remove from heat; cool.

Add powdered sugar and vanilla; beat on medium speed of electric mixer about 1 minute or until smooth and creamy. Add a small amount of milk to obtain spreading consistency, if necessary. Spread immediately on cake. Yield: enough for one 13- x 9-inch cake.

SCOTCH SPICE CAKE

½ cup quick-cooking oats, uncooked
⅓ cup boiling water
¾ cup evaporated milk
½ cup shortening
¼ cup sugar
1 cup firmly packed brown sugar
2 eggs
1¼ cups all-purpose flour, divided
½ teaspoon baking soda
½ teaspoon salt
½ teaspoon ground cinnamon
½ teaspoon ground cloves
½ cup raisins
½ cup chopped pecans

Combine oats, water, and milk; set aside. Cream shortening; gradually add sugar, beating well. Add eggs, one at a time, beating well after each addition.

Combine 1 cup flour, soda, salt, cinnamon, and cloves; add to creamed mixture alternately with oat mixture, beginning and ending with flour mixture. Dredge raisins and chopped pecans in remaining ¼ cup flour; stir into batter.

Pour batter into a greased and floured 9-inch square pan. Bake at 350° for 50 minutes or until a wooden pick inserted in center comes out clean. Cool. Cut into squares to serve. Yield: one 9-inch cake.

MOTHER'S ALWAYS FRESH AND SWEET CRUSHED OATS

The Quaker Oats Company

WATERMELON CAKE

White part: One teacupful of butter and milk, two teacupfuls sugar, three and one half teacupfuls flour, 3 teaspoonfuls baking powder, 1 teaspoonful extract of lemon and the whites of 8 eggs. Red part: One cupful red sugar, ½ cupful butter, ⅓ cupful milk, 2 cupfuls flour, 2 teaspoonfuls baking powder, and a teacupful raisins: bake in a pan with a tube in the center. Place the red part around the center of the pan and the white around the outside of this. Frost when done.

The Household Guide: A Complete Cookbook, by Mrs. J.L. Nichols, 1896

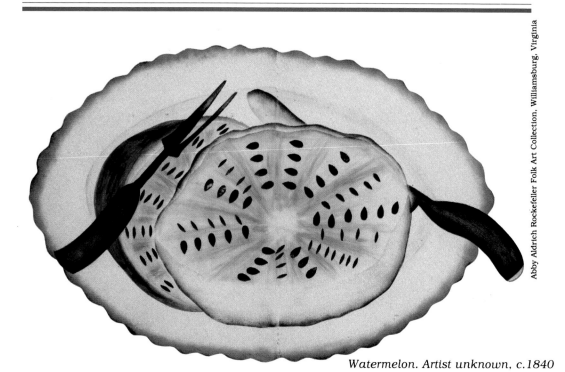

Abby Aldrich Rockefeller Folk Art Collection, Williamsburg, Virginia

Watermelon. Artist unknown, c.1840

RED WATERMELON CAKE

½ cup shortening
1½ cups sugar
2 eggs
3 tablespoons water
1 tablespoon red food coloring
1 tablespoon cocoa
2½ cups all-purpose flour
½ teaspoon salt
1 cup buttermilk
1½ teaspoons vinegar
1 teaspoon baking soda
1 cup raisins
Frosting (recipe follows)

Cream shortening; gradually add sugar, beating well. Add eggs, one at a time, beating well after each addition. Combine water, red food coloring, and cocoa; add to creamed mixture, beating well.

Combine flour and salt; add to creamed mixture alternately with buttermilk, beginning and ending with flour mixture. Combine vinegar and soda, stirring well; stir into batter. Fold raisins into batter.

Pour batter into 2 greased and floured 9-inch round cakepans. Bake at 350° for 35 to 40 minutes or until a wooden pick inserted in center comes out clean. Cool in pans 10 minutes; remove layers from pans, and let cool completely. Spread frosting between layers and on top and sides of cooled cake. Yield: one 2-layer cake.

Frosting:

¼ cup plus 1 tablespoon all-purpose flour
1 cup sugar
1 cup evaporated milk
1 cup butter or margarine
1 teaspoon vanilla extract
10 drops green food coloring

Combine flour, sugar, evaporated milk, and butter in a medium saucepan; cook over medium heat, stirring constantly, about 20 minutes or until thickened.

Stir in vanilla and green food coloring. Cool. Yield: enough for one 2-layer cake.

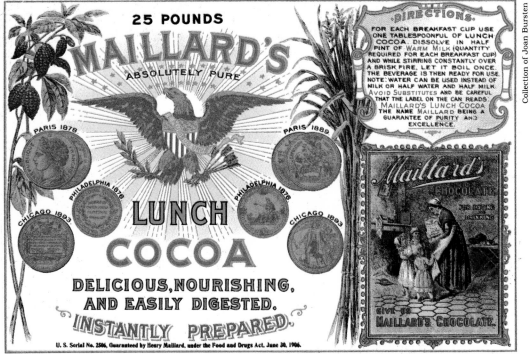

First manufactured in America in 1765, "eating" chocolate was developed in 1876.

CHOCOLATE MIDGETS

1½ cups sugar
1½ cups all-purpose flour, divided
½ teaspoon baking powder
1 cup butter or margarine
1 cup chocolate syrup
4 eggs, beaten
2 teaspoons vanilla extract
2 cups chopped pecans

Combine sugar, 1 cup flour, and baking powder; mix well and set aside.

Combine butter and chocolate syrup in a heavy saucepan; bring to a boil, stirring constantly. Remove from heat and cool. Gradually stir into flour mixture. Stir in eggs and vanilla. Dredge pecans in remaining ½ cup flour; stir into batter.

Pour batter into a greased and floured 9-inch square pan. Bake at 350° for 55 to 60 minutes or until a wooden pick inserted in center comes out clean. Cool in pan 10 minutes; cut into squares to serve. Yield: one 9-inch cake.

CHOCOLATE "FAILURE" CAKE

½ cup boiling water
2 tablespoons cocoa
1 teaspoon baking soda
½ cup shortening
2 cups sugar
2 eggs
2 cups all-purpose flour
1½ cups buttermilk
1 teaspoon vanilla extract
1 cup chopped pecans
Drippy Icing

Combine water, cocoa, and soda, stirring well. Set aside.

Cream shortening; gradually add sugar, beating well. Add eggs, one at a time, beating well after each addition.

Add flour to creamed mixture alternately with buttermilk, beginning and ending with flour. Stir in chocolate mixture, vanilla, and pecans.

Pour batter into a greased and waxed paper-lined 13- x 9- x 2-inch baking pan. Bake at 425° for 30 minutes or until a wooden pick inserted in center comes out clean. Cool cake completely. Pour Drippy Icing over top of cake. Cut cake into squares to serve. Yield: one 13- x 9-inch cake.

Drippy Icing:

1 teaspoon butter
1 cup sugar
3 tablespoons all-purpose flour
1½ cups milk
⅛ teaspoon vanilla extract

Combine all ingredients in a medium saucepan; bring to a boil, stirring constantly. Continue to cook over medium heat, stirring constantly, until mixture is thickened. Cool icing slightly. Yield: enough for one 13- x 9-inch cake.

Note: New to cake-baking? Begin your career with Chocolate "Failure" Cake. The cake is programmed to split open, the icing guaranteed to drip. It will be a triumphant beginning.

CHOCOLATE SHEATH CAKE

2 cups all-purpose flour
2 cups sugar
1 cup water
½ cup butter or margarine
½ cup shortening
¼ cup cocoa
½ cup buttermilk
2 eggs
1 teaspoon baking soda
1 teaspoon ground cinnamon
1 teaspoon vanilla extract
Chocolate-Peanut Frosting

Combine flour and sugar in a large mixing bowl; set aside.

Combine water, butter, shortening, and cocoa in a heavy saucepan; bring to a boil. Pour chocolate mixture over flour mixture; blend well. Add next 5 ingredients; mix well.

Pour batter into a lightly greased 13- x 9- x 2-inch baking pan. Bake at 400° for 25 minutes or until a wooden pick inserted in center comes out clean. Cool. Spread Chocolate-Peanut Frosting over cake. Yield: one 13- x 9-inch cake.

Chocolate-Peanut Frosting:

¼ cup cocoa
½ cup butter or margarine
¼ cup plus 2 tablespoons milk
1 (16-ounce) package powdered sugar, sifted
1 cup salted peanuts, chopped
1 cup flaked coconut (optional)
1 teaspoon vanilla extract

Combine cocoa, butter, and milk in a heavy saucepan; bring to a boil, stirring constantly. Remove from heat; stir in powdered sugar, peanuts, and coconut, if desired. Mix well and stir in vanilla. Yield: enough for one 13- x 9-inch cake.

Please everyone: Frost one cake with chocolate, another with vanilla.

After Cortez brought chocolate back to Spain from Mexico in the early 16th century, it became an overnight sensation. Actually, Spaniards were so mad for it that it was dubbed "addictive" and outlawed in parts of Spain.

In addition to its use as a beverage, chocolate was considered a medicine and was used to cure spasms, obesity, and a host of other ills. It was not until the early 1800s that chocolate began to appear as an ingredient in food.

MISSISSIPPI MUD CAKE

½ cup butter, softened
1 cup sugar
3 eggs
¾ cup all-purpose flour
½ teaspoon baking powder
Dash of salt
¼ cup plus 1½ tablespoons cocoa
1 teaspoon vanilla extract
1 cup chopped pecans
1 (10-ounce) package marshmallows
Chocolate Frosting

Cream butter; gradually add sugar, beating well. Add eggs, one at a time, beating well after each addition. Combine flour, baking powder, salt, and cocoa; add to creamed mixture. Stir in vanilla and pecans.

Spoon batter into a greased 13- x 9- x 2-inch glass baking pan. Bake at 325° for 15 to 18 minutes or until top is barely soft to the touch.

Remove cake from oven and cover top with marshmallows.

Return to oven for 2 minutes or until marshmallows are soft. Spread marshmallows over cake and immediately cover with Chocolate Frosting. Let frosting harden before cutting the cake into squares. Yield: one 13- x 9-inch cake.

Chocolate Frosting:

¼ cup butter or margarine
¼ cup plus 2 tablespoons cocoa
¼ cup plus 3 tablespoons warm milk
1 teaspoon vanilla extract
1 (16-ounce) package powdered sugar, sifted

Cream butter; add cocoa, mixing well. Gradually beat in powdered sugar, adding warm milk as necessary, until spreading consistency. Stir in vanilla. Spread immediately over warm marshmallows. Yield: enough for one 13- x 9-inch cake.

Marshmallows not just a treat, but an ingredient.

HOT WATER CHOCOLATE CAKE

⅔ cup butter or margarine, softened
2 cups sugar
2 eggs
4 (1-ounce) squares unsweetened chocolate, melted
2½ cups sifted cake flour
2 teaspoons baking powder
2 teaspoons baking soda
2 cups boiling water
2 teaspoons vanilla extract
Dark Fudge Frosting

Cream butter in a large mixing bowl; gradually add sugar, beating well. Add eggs, one at a time, beating well after each addition. Add chocolate, beating well.

Combine flour, baking powder, and soda; add to creamed mixture alternately with boiling water, beginning and ending with flour mixture. Beat well after each addition. Gently stir in vanilla.

Pour batter into a greased and floured 13- x 9- x 2-inch baking pan. Bake at 350° for 35 minutes or until a wooden pick inserted in center comes out clean. Cool 10 minutes. Turn out on a flat surface, and cool completely. Spread Dark Fudge Frosting on top and sides of cake. Yield: one 13- x 9-inch cake.

Dark Fudge Frosting:

2 cups sugar
½ cup cocoa
½ cup milk
¼ cup plus 2 tablespoons butter or margarine, softened
2 tablespoons light corn syrup
1 teaspoon vanilla extract

Combine all ingredients, except vanilla, in a heavy saucepan; bring to a boil, and cook 1 minute, stirring constantly. Remove from heat, and stir in vanilla. Cool slightly. Beat until spreading consistency. Spread immediately over cooled cake. Yield: enough for one 13- x 9-inch cake.

JIFFY CHOCOLATE CAKE

2 cups all-purpose flour
2 cups sugar
1 teaspoon baking soda
½ cup butter or margarine
½ cup vegetable oil
1 cup water
¼ cup chocolate syrup
⅓ cup buttermilk
2 eggs, beaten
1 teaspoon vanilla extract
Chocolate Frosting

Combine flour, sugar, and soda in a large mixing bowl, and set aside.

Combine butter, oil, water, and chocolate syrup in a medium saucepan; bring to a boil, stirring constantly. Gradually stir into flour mixture. Stir in buttermilk, eggs, and vanilla. Pour into a greased 15- x 10- x 1-inch jellyroll pan.

Bake at 400° for 20 minutes or until a wooden pick inserted in center comes out clean. Cool completely, and spread with Chocolate Frosting. Yield: one 15- x 10-inch cake.

Chocolate Frosting:

½ cup butter or margarine
⅓ cup evaporated milk
¼ cup chocolate syrup
1 (16-ounce) package
    powdered sugar, sifted
1 teaspoon vanilla extract
1 cup chopped pecans

Combine butter, milk, and chocolate syrup in a medium saucepan; bring to a boil, stirring constantly. Remove from heat; gradually add sugar, beating well. Stir in remaining ingredients. Yield: enough for one 15- x 10-inch cake.

*For Fine Cakes –
of Delicate Flavor.*

Collection of Business Americana

*From
an early
oleomargarine
recipe booklet*

OLD-FASHIONED CHEWY FUDGE CAKE

2 cups sugar
1 cup all-purpose flour
½ teaspoon salt
4 (1-ounce) squares
    unsweetened chocolate
½ cup butter or margarine
4 eggs, beaten
1 teaspoon vanilla extract
1 cup chopped pecans

Combine sugar, flour, and salt in a medium mixing bowl; mix well, and set aside.

Melt chocolate and butter over hot water in top of a double boiler, stirring well. Gradually stir chocolate mixture into flour mixture. Stir in eggs, vanilla, and chopped pecans.

Pour batter into a greased 13- x 9- x 2-inch baking pan. Bake at 325° for 40 to 45 minutes or until a wooden pick inserted in center comes out clean. Cool. Cut into squares to serve. Yield: one 13- x 9-inch cake.

BUSY DAY SYRUP CAKE

½ cup shortening
1½ cups cane syrup
2 eggs
2 cups all-purpose flour
1 teaspoon baking soda
½ teaspoon salt
½ cup cocoa
⅔ cup milk
1 teaspoon vanilla extract
Easy Chocolate Frosting

Cream shortening; gradually add syrup, beating until smooth. Add eggs one at a time, beating well after each addition.

Combine flour, soda, salt, and cocoa; add to creamed mixture alternately with milk, beginning and ending with flour mixture. Stir in vanilla.

Pour batter into 2 greased and floured 9-inch round cakepans. Bake at 350° for 25 to 30 minutes or until a wooden pick inserted in center comes out clean. Cool in pans 10 minutes; remove layers from pans and cool completely.

Spread Easy Chocolate Frosting between layers and on top and sides of cake. Yield: one 2-layer cake.

Easy Chocolate Frosting:

½ cup butter or margarine
¼ cup cocoa
¼ cup plus 2 tablespoons milk
4 to 5 cups sifted powdered sugar
1 teaspoon vanilla

Combine butter, cocoa, and milk in a medium saucepan. Bring to a boil over low heat, stirring constantly. Remove from heat and cool. Gradually add sugar, beating well until spreading consistency. Stir in vanilla. Yield: enough for one 2-layer cake.

Busy Day Syrup Cake, sweetened with cane syrup

WACKY CAKE

2 cups sugar
3 cups all-purpose flour
¼ cup plus 2 tablespoons cocoa
2 teaspoons baking soda
Pinch of salt
1 tablespoon vanilla extract
2 tablespoons vinegar
1¾ cups butter or margarine, softened
2 cups cold water
Caramel Frosting

Combine first 5 ingredients in a large bowl. Add vanilla, vinegar, and butter; beat well. Slowly stir in water; beat well.

Pour batter into an ungreased 13- x 9- x 2-inch baking pan. Bake at 350° for 35 to 40 minutes or until a wooden pick inserted in center comes out clean. Cool. Spread Caramel Frosting over cake. Yield: one 13- x 9-inch cake.

Caramel Frosting:

1½ cups firmly packed brown sugar
¼ cup plus 2 tablespoons milk
¼ cup plus 2 tablespoons shortening
¼ teaspoon salt
½ teaspoon vanilla extract

Combine all ingredients in a medium saucepan; bring to a boil and cook for 1 minute. Remove from heat; beat on medium speed of electric mixer about 10 minutes or until spreading consistency. Spread frosting on cake immediately. Yield: enough for one 13- x 9-inch cake.

LITTLE TREATS

CAKE FINGERS

½ cup butter, softened
1 cup sugar
1 egg, separated
2 cups all-purpose flour
¼ teaspoon salt
1 teaspoon ground cinnamon
2 tablespoons bourbon
  whiskey
1 teaspoon vanilla extract
2 cups chopped pecans

Cream butter; gradually add sugar, beating well. Add egg yolk; mix well.

Combine flour, salt, and cinnamon; add to creamed mixture alternately with bourbon, beginning and ending with flour mixture. Stir in vanilla. (Batter will be thick.)

Press dough evenly in a greased 13- x 9- x 2-inch baking pan. Brush with egg white, and sprinkle with chopped nuts. Bake at 350° for 45 minutes or until lightly browned. Cool in pan 5 minutes; cut into bars. Yield: about 2 dozen.

J umbles (jumbals) appeared in cookbooks in the 1700s. Jumbles have an interesting etymology: jumbal comes from gimbal, meaning a finger ring. The 1831 *Virginia Housewife* says simply, "knead all well together and bake." But *Housekeeping in the Bluegrass*, 1875, contains one which is rolled and cut into rounds with a hole. Our version is even easier, for no rolling is involved.

PEANUT-APPLE SQUARES

¼ cup butter or margarine,
  softened
1 cup sugar
½ cup peanut butter
1 egg
1¼ cups all-purpose flour
1 teaspoon baking soda
½ teaspoon salt
½ teaspoon ground cinnamon
¼ teaspoon ground nutmeg
¼ teaspoon ground cloves
1 cup applesauce

Cream butter; gradually add sugar, beating well. Add peanut butter and egg; beat well.

Combine flour, soda, salt, cinnamon, nutmeg, and cloves; add to creamed mixture alternately with applesauce, beginning and ending with flour mixture. Pour batter into a greased 8-inch square pan. Bake at 350° for 40 minutes or until a wooden pick inserted in center comes out clean. Cool in pan 10 minutes, and cut into squares. Yield: about sixteen 2-inch squares.

MAMAW'S CONFEDERATE JUMBLES

¾ cup butter, softened
1 cup sugar
1 egg
2 cups all-purpose flour
1 tablespoon baking powder
⅛ teaspoon salt
2 tablespoons buttermilk
1 teaspoon vanilla extract

Cream butter; gradually add sugar, beating until light and fluffy. Add egg; beat well.

Combine flour, baking powder, and salt; add to creamed mixture alternately with buttermilk, beginning and ending with flour mixture. Gently stir in vanilla.

Drop batter by heaping teaspoonfuls onto ungreased cookie sheets. Bake at 350° for 12 minutes or until lightly browned. Cool on wire racks. Yield: 5 dozen.

MIX-EASY CUPCAKES

½ cup shortening
1 cup sugar
2 cups sifted cake flour
2½ teaspoons baking
　powder
½ teaspoon salt
3 egg yolks, beaten
¾ cup milk
1 teaspoon vanilla extract

　Cream shortening; gradually add sugar, beating well.

　Sift together flour, baking powder, and salt. Combine egg yolks, milk, and vanilla. Add flour mixture to creamed mixture alternately with egg yolk mixture, beginning and ending with flour mixture; beat on medium speed of electric mixer for 3 minutes.

　Spoon batter into greased muffin pans, filling half full. Bake at 375° for 20 minutes or until cupcakes test done. Cool in pans 10 minutes; remove from pans, and cool completely. If desired, spread any frosting over tops of cupcakes. Yield: 2 dozen cupcakes.

BROWNIE CUPCAKES

4 (1-ounce) squares
　unsweetened chocolate
1 cup butter or margarine
¼ teaspoon butter extract
1½ cups chopped pecans
1 cup all-purpose flour
1¾ cups sugar
4 eggs, beaten
1 teaspoon vanilla extract
Powdered sugar (optional)

　Melt chocolate and margarine over low heat in a medium saucepan. Add butter extract and chopped pecans; stir well. Remove from heat, and set mixture aside.

　Combine flour, sugar, eggs, and vanilla in a large mixing bowl; add chocolate mixture, and stir until moistened.

　Spoon 3 tablespoons batter each into paper-lined muffin pans. Bake at 325° for 30 to 35 minutes or until cupcakes test done. Cool in pan 10 minutes; remove to wire rack to cool completely. Sprinkle with powdered sugar, if desired. Yield: 1½ dozen cupcakes.

ORANGE CUPCAKES

½ cup shortening
1 cup sugar
2 eggs
1 teaspoon baking soda
⅔ cup buttermilk
2 cups all-purpose flour,
　divided
½ teaspoon salt
1 cup chopped dates
1 cup chopped pecans
Orange Syrup

　Cream shortening; gradually add sugar, beating well. Add eggs, one at a time, beating well after each addition.

　Dissolve soda in buttermilk, stirring well. Combine 1½ cups flour and salt; add to creamed mixture alternately with buttermilk mixture, beginning and ending with flour mixture. Combine dates and pecans; dredge in remaining ½ cup flour, and fold into batter.

　Spoon batter into greased muffin pans, filling only two-thirds full. Bake at 375° for 12 to 14 minutes or until cupcakes test done. Spoon Orange Syrup over cupcakes. Yield: about 1½ dozen cupcakes.

Orange Syrup:

½ cup sugar
1½ teaspoon grated orange
　rind
½ cup orange juice

　Combine all ingredients in a heavy saucepan. Bring to a boil, stirring constantly until sugar dissolves. Yield: ¾ cup.

Brownie Cupcakes and Orange Cupcakes are popular pickup snacks. Cupcakes were baked in cups before muffin irons or tins were available.

DELICATE CUPCAKES

½ cup butter or margarine,
　softened
1 cup sugar
2 eggs
2 cups all-purpose flour
2 teaspoons baking powder
¼ teaspoon salt
⅔ cup milk
1 teaspoon vanilla extract
Vanilla Butter Frosting
Flaked coconut

　Cream butter; gradually add sugar, beating well. Add eggs, one at a time, beating well after each addition.

　Combine flour, baking powder, and salt; add to creamed mixture alternately with milk, beginning and ending with the flour mixture. Stir in vanilla.

　Spoon batter into greased and floured muffin pans, filling only two-thirds full. Bake at 375° for 20 minutes or until cupcakes test done. Cool and frost with Vanilla Butter Frosting. Sprinkle flaked coconut over top. Yield: 1½ dozen cupcakes.

Vanilla Butter Frosting:

¼ cup plus 1½ teaspoons
　butter, softened
2¼ cups sifted powdered
　sugar, divided
1½ tablespoons milk
1½ teaspoons vanilla extract

　Combine butter and ½ cup sugar, creaming with electric mixer until light and fluffy. Add remaining sugar alternately with milk, beating until spreading consistency. Add vanilla; beat well. Yield: enough for 1½ dozen cupcakes.

CELEBRATION CAKES

While it may not be exactly true that Southerners have more fun than folks in other parts of the country, still we wear an air of hubris that can border on zaniness at times of great celebrations. Ask why and we may say, tongue firmly in cheek, that we did not have the advantage of an upbringing rooted in puritanism. Or we might claim our salubrious climate has something to do with it, though parts of the South are less than perfect in that regard. Whatever the reasoning behind our commitment to celebrations, you'd have to be there in order to understand our zest for them.

The biggest and most celebrated Southern festival is Mardi Gras. New Orleans natives and visitors alike exhaust themselves in the pre-Lenten madness that lasts for weeks. Great balls are given all over the city, but the tradition of the King Cake is never omitted.

The King Cake is made of yeast dough baked in the shape of a crown and bejewelled with candied fruits, silver and gold dragées . . . whatever the baker fancies. Hidden inside is a dried bean or a pecan half. The finder becomes king or queen for a week and is responsible for bringing another King Cake for the next party.

On a more personal scale are the cakes for celebration of family occasions such as birthdays, weddings, and Christmas. The French yule log, Bûche de Noël, is as much a holiday tradition in many Southern families as fruitcake is in others. Many of our fruitcakes are patterned after the Great Cake Martha Washington served, but few of us have ever seen one of such gargantuan proportions as the original.

A fruitcake will keep well for quite a long time if properly handled: For storage, it must be wrapped in cloth soaked in brandy or bourbon, then wrapped with plastic or waxed paper, and placed in a tightly covered tin. Spirits must be added from time to time to moisten the cloth. Never use aluminum foil to wrap; alcohol will make holes in it. Fruit juice won't work; it is alcohol that preserves the cake.

Brides' cakes have also been scaled down over the past century. An 1883 recipe for a wedding cake makes "forty-three and a half pounds, and keeps twenty years." Would it not make more sense to start out with a longer guest list? No matter; whatever the occasion, celebrate it with a cake.

A festive array of Christmas cakes. Clockwise from front right: White Fruitcake (page 92), Southern Fruitcake (page 93), Brazil Nut Cake (page 90), and Blue Ribbon White Cake (page 93) glazed with marshmallow icing.

MARTHA WASHINGTON'S GREAT CAKE

- 1 (15-ounce) package golden raisins
- 1 (10-ounce) package currants
- 2 (4-ounce) packages chopped candied orange peel
- 2 (4-ounce) packages chopped candied citron
- ¾ cup chopped candied lemon peel
- ⅓ cup candied red cherries, chopped
- ⅓ cup candied green cherries, chopped
- ⅓ cup candied angelica, chopped (optional)
- ½ cup brandy
- 2 cups butter or margarine, softened
- 2 cups sugar
- 10 eggs, separated
- 2 teaspoons lemon juice
- 4½ cups all-purpose flour
- 1 teaspoon ground mace
- ½ teaspoon ground nutmeg
- ⅓ cup sherry
- Candied red cherries
- Angelica (optional)

Combine first 9 ingredients; stir well. Let stand overnight.

Cream butter in a large mixing bowl; gradually add sugar, beating until light and fluffy. Add egg yolks, one at a time, beating well after each addition. Stir in lemon juice.

Combine flour, mace, and nutmeg; add to creamed mixture alternately with sherry, beginning and ending with flour mixture. Mix well after each addition. Stir in reserved fruit mixture.

Beat egg whites (at room temperature) until stiff peaks form; fold into batter.

Spoon batter into a well-greased and floured 10-inch tube pan. Place a large pan of boiling water on lower oven rack. Bake cake at 350° for 20 minutes; reduce temperature to 325°, and bake an additional 1 hour and 40 minutes or until cake tests done.

Cool cake completely in pan. Remove from pan, and garnish with candied red cherries and angelica, if desired. Yield: one 10-inch cake.

The Mount Vernon Collection

Above: Portrait of Martha Washington by Charles Willson Peale, 1776

Right: Receipt for a "Great Cake," written out for Mrs. Washington by her granddaughter, Martha Custis.

BRAZIL NUT CAKE

- 2 cups chopped Brazil nuts
- 2 (8-ounce) packages pitted, imported dates, chopped
- 1 cup chopped pecans
- 1 cup chopped maraschino cherries
- ¾ cup all-purpose flour
- ¾ cup sugar
- ½ teaspoon baking powder
- ½ teaspoon salt
- 3 eggs, beaten
- 1 teaspoon vanilla extract

Combine first 4 ingredients; stir well. Combine dry ingredients, stir into fruit mixture. Add eggs and vanilla; mix well.

Spoon batter into a greased and waxed paper-lined 8½- x 4½- x 3-inch loafpan. Bake at 300° for 1 hour and 45 minutes or until a wooden pick inserted in center comes out clean. Cool in pan 10 minutes; remove from pan, and cool completely. Yield: 1 loaf.

Mount Vernon Ladies' Association

JAMES K. POLK FRUITCAKE

¼ cup blanched almonds, chopped
¼ cup orange juice
1 cup butter, softened
1 cup sugar
6 eggs
2 cups all-purpose flour, divided
1½ teaspoons ground cinnamon
½ teaspoon ground cloves
½ teaspoon ground nutmeg
½ teaspoon ground allspice
½ teaspoon ground mace
1 cup orange juice
4½ cups raisins
2 (8-ounce) packages chopped dates
1½ cups currants
2 (4-ounce) packages chopped candied citron
1½ cups chopped candied pineapple
1½ cups chopped pecans

Grease four 7½- x 3- x 2-inch loaf pans, and line the sides and bottom with greased heavy brown paper. Set aside.

Combine almonds and ¼ cup orange juice; set aside.

Cream butter in a large mixing bowl; gradually add sugar, beating until light and fluffy. Add eggs, one at a time, beating well after each addition.

Combine 1½ cups flour, cinnamon, cloves, nutmeg, allspice, and mace; add to creamed mixture alternately with 1 cup orange juice, beginning and ending with flour mixture. Mix well after each addition.

Dredge remaining ingredients in ½ cup flour; gently stir into batter. Add almond mixture, stirring well.

Spoon batter into prepared pans. Bake at 300° for 1 hour and 30 minutes or until a wooden pick inserted in center comes out clean. Cool cakes completely in pans. Yield: 4 loaves.

Daguerreotype (1840s) during Polk's administration. Eleventh President and Mrs. Polk at center. Extreme left: Secretary of State James Buchanan and his niece. Second from right: Dolley Madison. By now in her 70s, Mrs. Madison had married James Madison in 1794. Although a Southerner by birth, Dorothy Payne Todd, nicknamed Dolley, came from Pennsylvania Quaker stock.

Moving with her husband to his Montpeller estate in Virginia, Dolley quickly took to plantation life, gaining a reputation for high style in her dress and entertaining.

Daguerreotype during Polk administration

SHENANDOAH INDIVIDUAL FRUITCAKES

¼ cup plus 1 tablespoon
  butter or margarine
2 cups sugar
1½ cups water
1 cup raisins
1 (8-ounce) package chopped
  dates
3 cups all-purpose flour,
  divided
1 teaspoon baking soda
¾ teaspoon salt
1 teaspoon ground cinnamon
½ teaspoon ground cloves
2 eggs
2 (8-ounce) packages chopped
  candied mixed fruit
1 cup chopped pecans
Whole pecans (optional)

Place butter, sugar, water, raisins, and dates in a saucepan; cook on low heat about 10 minutes. Remove from heat, and let mixture cool completely. Set aside.

Combine 2 cups flour, soda, salt, cinnamon, and cloves. Add flour mixture to date mixture; stir well. Add eggs, mixing well.

Dredge candied mixed fruit and pecans with remaining 1 cup flour; add to batter, mixing well. Spoon batter into greased and floured muffin pans, filling two-thirds full. Place a whole pecan on top of each muffin, if desired. Bake at 275° for 1 hour and 10 minutes or until cakes test done. Yield: about 2½ dozen.

Label for a box of raisins, c.1900

WHITE FRUITCAKE

1 (16-ounce) package candied
  red cherries, finely chopped
1 (4-ounce) package candied
  red cherries, finely chopped
1 (16-ounce) package
  candied pineapple, finely
  chopped
1 (4-ounce) package candied
  pineapple, finely chopped
3 cups chopped pecans
1¼ cups golden raisins
3½ cups sifted cake flour,
  divided

1 cup butter, softened
2¼ cups sugar
6 eggs
¼ teaspoon baking soda
2 tablespoons lemon juice
1½ teaspoons vanilla extract

Combine first 6 ingredients; dredge with 1 cup flour, stirring to coat well. Set aside.

Cream butter in large mixing bowl; gradually add sugar, beating well. Add eggs, one at a time, beating well after each addition.

Combine remaining 2½ cups flour and soda. Gradually add flour mixture to creamed mixture, mixing well. Stir in dredged fruit mixture, lemon juice, and vanilla.

Spoon batter into a well-greased 10-inch tube pan. Bake at 275° for 3½ to 4 hours or until cake tests done. Cool cake completely in pan. Yield: one 10-inch cake.

SOUTHERN FRUITCAKE

2 (15-ounce) packages raisins, chopped
2 (4-ounce) packages chopped candied citron
1 (8-ounce) package candied red cherries, finely chopped
1 (8-ounce) package chopped candied pineapple
1 (4-ounce) package chopped candied lemon peel
1 (4-ounce) package chopped candied orange peel
1 cup chopped pecans
¾ cup chopped almonds
½ cup white wine
1 cup butter or margarine, softened
1 cup sugar
½ cup grape jelly
5 eggs
1¾ cups all-purpose flour
1½ tablespoons ground cinnamon
¼ teaspoon ground allspice
¼ teaspoon ground nutmeg
⅛ teaspoon ground cloves
1 teaspoon vanilla extract
¼ teaspoon lemon extract
¼ teaspoon orange extract

Combine first 9 ingredients; let stand overnight.

Cream butter in a large mixing bowl; gradually add sugar, beating until light and fluffy. Add jelly, beating well. Add eggs, one at a time, beating well after each addition.

Combine flour and spices; add to creamed mixture, mixing well. Stir in fruit mixture and flavorings.

Spoon batter into a brown paper-lined and greased 10-inch tube pan. Bake at 275° for 3 to 3½ hours or until cake tests done. Cool cake completely in pan. Yield: one 10-inch cake.

Mrs. W.E. Farley, after winning twenty blue ribbons at Kentucky State Fairs for her cakes. She gave all the credit to Calumet Baking Powder.

BLUE RIBBON WHITE CAKE

1 cup butter, softened
2 cups sugar
3 cups sifted cake flour
2 tablespoons baking powder
1 cup half-and-half
8 egg whites
Marshmallow Glaze
Candied cherries

Cream butter; gradually add sugar, beating well.

Combine flour and baking powder; add to creamed mixture alternately with half-and-half, beginning and ending with the flour mixture.

Beat egg whites (at room temperature) until stiff peaks form; fold into batter.

Pour batter into a greased 10-inch Bundt pan. Bake at 350° for 1 hour or until cake tests done. Cool in pan 10 minutes; remove from pan, and cool completely. Drizzle Marshmallow Glaze over cake, and garnish with candied cherries. Yield: one 10-inch cake.

Marshmallow Glaze:

1 cup sugar
⅓ cup water
5 large marshmallows, chopped
1 egg white
Pinch of cream of tartar
1 teaspoon almond extract

Combine sugar and water in a medium saucepan. Cook over medium heat, stirring frequently, until mixture comes to a boil and sugar is dissolved.

Continue cooking, stirring frequently, until mixture reaches soft ball stage (240°). Add marshmallows; cook 1 minute or until blended, stirring mixture frequently.

Combine egg white and cream of tartar; beat until foamy. While beating at medium speed of electric mixer, slowly pour hot syrup mixture in a thin stream over egg white. Add almond extract; mix well. Turn mixer to high speed, and continue beating until stiff peaks form and glaze is thickened. Yield: enough for one 10-inch cake.

Irresistible Bûche de Noël, the classic French yule log

BÛCHE DE NOËL

4 eggs
¾ teaspoon baking powder
¼ teaspoon salt
¾ cup sugar
¾ cup all-purpose flour
¼ cup cocoa
1 teaspoon vanilla extract
2 to 3 tablespoons powdered
 sugar
2 cups sweetened whipped
 cream
1 tablespoon instant coffee
 granules
⅓ cup boiling water
3 (1-ounce) squares
 unsweetened chocolate
¼ cup butter or margarine
Dash of salt
About 2½ cups sifted
 powdered sugar
Candied cherries

Grease a 15- x 10- x 1-inch jel-lyroll pan; line with waxed paper and grease lightly.

Combine first 3 ingredients; beat at medium speed of electric mixer. Gradually add ¾ cup sugar, beating until thick and light colored. Fold in flour, cocoa, and vanilla.

Spread mixture evenly into prepared pan. Bake at 400° for 13 minutes or until surface springs back when gently pressed.

Sift 2 to 3 tablespoons pow-dered sugar in a 15- x 10-inch rectangle on a linen towel. Turn cake out onto sugar; remove waxed paper from cake. Trim crisp edges, if necessary. Start-ing with the short end, carefully

roll cake and towel, jellyroll fash-ion. Cool thoroughly on wire rack. Unroll and remove towel; spread with whipped cream, and reroll. Chill.

Dissolve coffee granules in boiling water; stir well, and set aside.

Melt chocolate in top of a dou-ble boiler; add butter, coffee mixture, and salt, stirring until smooth. Cool to lukewarm. Stir in about 2½ cups sifted pow-dered sugar to make a spread-ing consistency.

Spread frosting evenly over cake. Mark with spatula or tines of a fork to resemble bark of a tree. Garnish with candied cherries. Refrigerate until serv-ing time. Yield: 8 to 10 servings.

94

SNOWBALL CAKE

1 cup butter or margarine,
softened
2 cups sugar
3½ cups all-purpose flour
2 teaspoons baking powder
⅛ teaspoon salt
1 cup milk
½ teaspoon vanilla extract
½ teaspoon lemon extract
5 egg whites
Fluffy White Frosting
About 4 cups flaked coconut

Cream butter; gradually add sugar, beating well.

Combine flour, baking powder, and salt; add to the creamed mixture alternately with milk, beginning and ending with the flour mixture. Mix well after each addition. Stir in the flavorings.

Beat egg whites (at room temperature) until stiff peaks form; fold into batter.

Pour batter into a greased and floured 13- x 9- x 2-inch baking pan. Bake at 350° for 45 minutes or until a wooden pick inserted in center comes out clean. Cool in pan 10 minutes; remove from pan, and let cool completely.

Cut cake into 2-inch squares; trim corners of each square, leaving rounded edges. Spread top and sides of each round with Fluffy White Frosting. Sprinkle coconut generously over frosting. Yield: 2 dozen.

Fluffy White Frosting:

1½ cups sugar
2 egg whites
1 tablespoon light corn syrup
¼ teaspoon cream of tartar
¼ cup plus 1 tablespoon cold water
1 teaspoon vanilla extract

Combine first 4 ingredients in top of a large double boiler; add cold water, and beat on low speed of electric mixer just until blended.

Place over boiling water; beat constantly on high speed about 3 minutes or until soft peaks form. Remove from heat, and place over cold water. Add vanilla; beat 3 additional minutes or until frosting is thick enough to spread. Yield: enough for 24 individual cakes.

Note: The flavor of Snowball Cakes will be enhanced if freshly grated coconut is substituted for flaked coconut.

WINE CAKES

1 cup butter or margarine,
softened
1¾ cups sugar
5 eggs
2 cups all-purpose flour
½ teaspoon almond extract
⅓ cup sherry
½ cup whipping cream, whipped
30 maraschino cherries with stems

Cream butter; gradually add sugar, beating until light and fluffy. Add eggs, one at a time, beating well after each addition. Gradually add flour, stirring well. Stir in almond extract.

Spoon batter into greased and floured muffin pans, filling half full. Bake at 350° for 20 to 25 minutes or until cupcakes test done. Cool in pans 10 minutes; remove from pans, and pour sherry evenly over cupcakes. Let set at least 30 minutes. Just before serving, top each cupcake with a dollop of whipped cream and a cherry. Yield: 2½ dozen cupcakes.

Winter scene from Ballou's Pictorial Drawingroom Companion, *1856*

FESTIVE OCCASIONS

NEW YEAR'S CARAWAY CAKES

1 cup butter or margarine, softened
1¼ cups sugar
1 egg
½ cup water
5¾ cups all-purpose flour
½ teaspoon baking soda
2 tablespoons caraway seeds

Cream butter; gradually add sugar, beating until light and fluffy. Add egg and water, beating well.

Combine flour, soda, and caraway seeds; add to creamed mixture, beating well. Chill dough 1 hour.

Roll dough out onto a lightly floured surface to ⅛-inch thickness; cut out with a 2-inch cookie cutter. Place on lightly greased cookie sheets. Bake at 400° for 8 to 10 minutes or until lightly browned. Store in airtight containers. Yield: about 4 dozen.

"I wonder if you know who this is from . . ." ran the opening line on this New Year's postcard mailed to a gentleman on December 31, 1909—presumably from a lady.

A Happy New Year

RED VALENTINE CAKE

½ cup butter, softened
1½ cups sugar
2 eggs
2 tablespoons hot coffee
2 tablespoons cocoa
1 teaspoon red food coloring
1 teaspoon baking soda
1 cup buttermilk
2 cups all-purpose flour
1 teaspoon salt
Toasted Pecan Topping

Cream butter; add sugar, beating well. Add eggs, one at a time, beating well after each addition. Combine next 3 ingredients; add to creamed mixture, beating well.

Dissolve soda in buttermilk, stirring well. Combine flour and salt; add to creamed mixture alternately with buttermilk mixture, beginning and ending with flour mixture.

Pour batter into 2 greased and floured 8-inch round cakepans. Bake at 325° for 35 minutes or until a wooden pick inserted in center comes out clean. Cool layers in pans 10 minutes; remove layers from pans, and let cool completely.

Spread Toasted Pecan Topping between layers and on top of cake. Yield: one 2-layer cake.

Toasted Pecan Topping:

2 tablespoons butter or margarine
1 cup chopped pecans
2 cups sifted powdered sugar
3 tablespoons whipping cream
1 teaspoon vanilla extract

Place butter and pecans in a 9-inch square pan. Bake at 200° for 15 to 20 minutes, stirring after 10 minutes. Drain on paper towels; set aside. Combine sugar, cream, and vanilla; beat until smooth. Stir in pecans. Yield: about 1 cup.

CREOLE VALENTINE CAKE

⅔ cup shortening
1½ cups sugar
3 cups sifted cake flour
1 tablespoon plus ½
　teaspoon baking powder
¾ teaspoon salt
1 cup milk
1 teaspoon almond extract
4 egg whites
½ cup chopped maraschino
　cherries, drained
¾ cup finely chopped
　blanched almonds
8 drops red food coloring
Frosting (recipe follows)
Halved maraschino cherries

Grease and flour three 8-inch heart-shaped cakepans.

Cream shortening; gradually add sugar, beating well.

Combine flour, baking powder, and salt; add to creamed mixture alternately with milk, beginning and ending with flour mixture. Mix well after each addition. Stir in flavoring.

Beat egg whites (at room temperature) until stiff peaks form; fold into batter.

Add cherries to one-third of batter, and pour into 1 prepared cakepan. Add almonds and food coloring to remaining batter, and pour into 2 remaining cakepans. Bake at 350° for 20 to 25 minutes or until cake tests done. Cool in pans 10 minutes; remove from pans, and let cool completely. Spread frosting between alternating pink and white layers and on top and sides of cake. Garnish with halved cherries. Yield: one 3-layer cake.

Frosting:

2 cups sugar
1 cup water
2 egg whites
2 to 3 drops red food coloring

Combine sugar and water in a medium-size heavy saucepan. Cook over medium heat, stirring frequently, until mixture comes to a boil and sugar is dissolved. Continue cooking, stirring frequently, until the mixture reaches soft ball stage (240°).

Beat egg whites (at room temperature) until foamy. While beating at medium speed of electric mixer, slowly pour hot syrup in a thin stream over egg whites. Turn mixer to high speed; continue beating until stiff peaks form and frosting is thick enough to spread. Add food coloring; beat until blended. Spread on cake immediately. Yield: enough for one 3-layer cake.

Creole Valentine Cake is for the sentimental season.

Mount Vernon, view of the west front with a family group on the bowling green, c.1792

MOUNT VERNON CAKE

1 cup shortening
2 cups sugar
4 eggs, separated
3 cups all-purpose flour
1 tablespoon baking powder
¼ teaspoon salt
1 cup milk
2 teaspoons vanilla extract
Cherry Filling
Seven-Minute Double Boiler
  Frosting
Maraschino cherries with
  stems

Cream shortening; gradually add sugar, beating well. Add egg yolks, and beat well.

Combine flour, baking powder, and salt; add to creamed mixture alternately with milk, beginning and ending with flour mixture. Mix well after each addition. Stir in vanilla.

Beat egg whites (at room temperature) until stiff peaks form; fold into batter.

Pour the batter into 3 greased and floured 8-inch round cake-pans. Bake at 350° for 25 to 30 minutes or until a wooden pick inserted in center comes out clean. Cool in pans 10 minutes; remove layers from pans, and let cool completely.

Spread Cherry Filling between layers; spread top and sides of cake with Seven-Minute Double Boiler Frosting. Arrange cherries on top of cake. Yield: one 3-layer cake.

Cherry Filling:

1 (16-ounce) can pitted tart
  red cherries, undrained
½ cup light corn syrup
¼ cup sugar
2½ tablespoons cornstarch
4 drops red food coloring
1 teaspoon almond extract

Drain cherries, reserving liquid (add water, if necessary, to make 1 cup). Set aside.

Combine corn syrup, sugar, and cornstarch in a small saucepan; stir well. Add reserved cherry liquid and food coloring; cook over medium heat, stirring constantly, until smooth and thickened. Stir in drained cherries and almond extract. Yield: about 2½ cups.

Seven-Minute Double Boiler Frosting:

1½ cups sugar
2 eggs whites
1 tablespoon light corn syrup
Dash of salt
⅓ cup cold water
1 teaspoon vanilla extract

Combine sugar, egg whites, corn syrup, and salt in top of a large double boiler; add cold water, and beat on low speed of electric mixer for 30 seconds.

Place over boiling water; beat constantly on high speed about 7 minutes or until stiff peaks form. Remove from heat. Add vanilla; beat 2 additional minutes or until thick enough to spread. Yield: enough for one 3-layer cake.

KING CAKE

½ cup warm water (105°
  to 115°)
2 packages dry yeast
2 teaspoons sugar
4 to 5 cups all-purpose flour
½ cup sugar
2 teaspoons salt
1 teaspoon ground nutmeg
1 teaspoon grated lemon rind
½ cup warm milk (105°
  to 115°)
½ cup melted butter, cooled
5 egg yolks
½ cup finely chopped candied
  citron (optional)
1 pecan half or uncooked
  dried bean
Glaze (recipe follows)
Purple, green, and gold sugar
  crystals

Combine warm water, yeast, and 2 teaspoons sugar in a small bowl. Mix well; set in a warm place about 10 minutes.

Combine 4 cups flour, ½ cup sugar, salt, nutmeg, and lemon rind; add warm milk, melted butter, egg yolks, and yeast mixture. Beat until smooth.

Turn dough out onto a lightly floured surface; knead in enough remaining flour until dough is no longer sticky. Continue kneading about 10 minutes until dough is smooth and elastic.

Place dough in a well-greased bowl, turning to grease top. Cover and let rise in a warm place (85°), free from drafts, about 1½ hours or until doubled in bulk.

Punch dough down, and place on a lightly floured surface. Sprinkle with citron, if desired, kneading until citron is evenly distributed. Shape dough into a cylinder 30 inches long.

Place cylinder on a buttered baking sheet; shape into a ring, pinching ends together to seal.

Place a well-greased 2-pound coffee can or shortening can in center of ring to maintain shape during baking.

Press pecan half gently into ring from bottom so it is completely hidden by dough. Cover and let rise in a warm place about 45 minutes or until doubled in bulk.

Bake at 350° for 30 minutes or until golden brown. Remove coffee can immediately. Allow cake to cool. Drizzle cake with glaze; sprinkle with sugar crystals, alternating colors. Yield: 1 coffee cake.

Glaze:

2 cups sifted powdered sugar
2 tablespoons lemon juice
2 tablespoons water

Combine all ingredients, and beat until smooth. Yield: about 1½ cups.

This postcard depicts a Mardi Gras parade in New Orleans, c.1928.

New York Public Library Picture Collection

EASTER ORANGE COCONUT CAKE

¾ cup shortening
1¾ cups sugar
2½ cups all-purpose flour
1½ tablespoons baking powder
1½ teaspoons salt
1 cup plus 2 tablespoons milk
1 teaspoon almond extract
5 egg whites
Orange Filling
Frosting (recipe follows)
About ¾ cup flaked coconut

Cream shortening; gradually add sugar, beating well.

Combine flour, baking powder, and salt; add to creamed mixture alternately with milk, beginning and ending with flour mixture. Mix well after each addition. Stir in flavoring.

Beat egg whites (at room temperature) until stiff but not dry; fold into batter.

Pour batter into 2 greased and floured 9-inch round cakepans. Bake at 350° for 35 to 40 minutes or until a wooden pick inserted in center comes out clean. Cool in pans 10 minutes; remove layers from pans, and let cool completely.

Spread Orange Filling between layers; spread top and sides of cake with frosting, and sprinkle with coconut. Yield: one 2-layer cake.

Orange Filling:

½ cup sugar
2 tablespoons butter
1½ teaspoons cornstarch
⅛ teaspoon salt
2 tablespoons orange rind
1½ tablespoons lemon juice

Combine first 5 ingredients in a medium saucepan; cook over medium heat, stirring constantly, until thickened. Remove from heat; stir in lemon juice. Yield: about 1 cup.

Frosting:

1½ cups sugar
½ cup water
½ teaspoon salt
3 egg whites
1½ teaspoons vanilla extract

Combine sugar, water, and salt in a medium saucepan. Cook over medium heat, stirring frequently, until mixture comes to a boil and sugar is dissolved. Continue cooking, stirring frequently, until the mixture reaches soft ball stage (240°).

Beat egg whites (at room temperature) until foamy. While beating at medium speed of electric mixer, slowly pour hot syrup in a thin stream over egg whites. Turn mixer to high speed; continue beating until stiff peaks form and frosting is thick enough to spread. Add vanilla; beat until blended. Yield: enough for one 2-layer cake.

In pre-Mosaic days, what is now celebrated as Passover may have been only a spring festival. But for orthodox Jews, it became a seven-day thanksgiving for their deliverance from Egypt. The seder dinner is symbolic of their bondage. Unleavened bread is eaten. Egg white lightens Passover sponge cake; fine, dry nut meal is used instead of flour.

Easter postcard, c.1900

PASSOVER CHOCOLATE SPONGE CAKE

6 (1-ounce) squares semisweet chocolate
10 eggs, separated
¾ cup plus 2 tablespoons sugar
2 cups finely grated almonds

Melt chocolate in top of a double boiler; set aside.

Beat egg yolks until thick and lemon colored. Gradually add sugar; beat well after each addition. Add chocolate and almonds; stir well.

Beat egg whites (at room temperature) until stiff peaks form. Fold whites into batter.

Spoon batter into an ungreased 10-inch tube pan. Bake at 350° for 1 hour or until cake springs back when lightly touched. Remove from oven; invert pan, and cool about 40 minutes before removing from pan. Yield: one 10-inch cake.

Note: Finely grated nuts are used instead of flour in this recipe. A hand grinder is preferable to a food processor or blender because electric machines bring out the oil in nuts. If a blender or food processor is used, grate only ½ cup at a time. Do not pack down when measuring.

NEAPOLITAN HALLOWEEN CAKE

1⅓ cups shortening
3 cups sugar
6 eggs, separated
5½ cups all-purpose flour
1 tablespoon plus 2
  teaspoons baking powder
1½ cups milk
2 teaspoons vanilla extract
4 (1-ounce) squares
  semisweet chocolate,
  melted
¼ cup all-purpose flour
10 drops yellow food coloring
5 drops red food coloring
Filling (recipe follows)
Chocolate Fudge Frosting

Cream shortening; gradually add sugar, beating well. Add egg yolks, one at a time, beating well after each addition.

Combine 5½ cups flour and baking powder; add to creamed mixture alternately with milk, beginning and ending with flour mixture. Mix well after each addition. Stir in vanilla.

Add chocolate to two-thirds of batter; mix well. Add ¼ cup flour and food coloring to the remaining one-third of batter; mix well.

Line three 9-inch round checkerboard cakepans with greased waxed paper; grease sides of pan. Place checkerboard divider rings into one prepared pan. Carefully spoon one-third of orange batter into center and outer rings; spoon one-third of chocolate batter into middle ring, filling half full (a pastry bag may be used to pipe batters into rings). Smooth batter with a small spatula. Carefully remove rings. Rinse rings, and dry thoroughly before placing in next pan. Repeat procedure with remaining batter and pans.

Bake at 350° for 30 minutes or until a wooden pick inserted in center comes out clean. Cool in pans 10 minutes; remove layers from pans, and let cool completely. Spread filling between layers. Spread top and sides of cake with Chocolate Fudge Frosting. Yield: one 3-layer cake.

Neapolitan Halloween Cake: baked in checkerboard cakepans

Filling:

1 cup sifted powdered sugar
1 to 2 tablespoons milk
½ teaspoon vanilla extract

Combine all ingredients, and beat until smooth. Yield: about ½ cup.

Chocolate Fudge Frosting:

½ cup butter or margarine
¾ cup half-and-half
6 (1-ounce) squares
  unsweetened chocolate
5 cups sifted powdered sugar
2 teaspoons vanilla extract

Combine butter, half-and-half, and chocolate in top of double boiler; cook over medium heat, stirring frequently, just until mixture comes to a boil. Remove from heat, and add sugar; beat until smooth. Stir in vanilla. Yield: enough for one 3-layer cake.

HALLOWEEN DATE FUDGE CAKE

½ cup butter, softened
1¼ cups firmly packed brown sugar
2 eggs
3 (1-ounce) squares unsweetened chocolate, melted
1¾ cups all-purpose flour, divided
1 teaspoon baking soda
½ teaspoon salt
1 cup milk
½ cup miniature marshmallows
1 cup chopped dates
1 teaspoon grated orange rind
1 cup chopped pecans
1 teaspoon vanilla extract
Orange Frosting

Cream butter; gradually add sugar, beating well. Add eggs, one at a time, beating well after each addition. Add chocolate, mixing well.

Combine 1½ cups flour, soda, and salt; gradually add to chocolate mixture alternately with milk, beginning and ending with flour mixture. Dredge marshmallows, dates, orange rind, and pecans with remaining ¼ cup flour; stir to coat well. Add date mixture and vanilla to batter; stir well.

Spoon batter into 2 greased 8½- x 4½- x 3-inch loafpans. Bake at 350° for 1 hour and 10 minutes or until a wooden pick inserted in center comes out clean. Let cool in pans 20 minutes; remove from pans, and place on wire racks to cool completely. Top with Orange Frosting. Yield: 2 loaves.

Orange Frosting:

¼ cup plus 2 tablespoons butter, softened
3 cups sifted powdered sugar
1 tablespoon plus 1 teaspoon grated orange rind
2 tablespoons orange juice
12 drops red food coloring
3 drops yellow food coloring

Combine all ingredients; beat until light and fluffy. Yield: enough for 2 loaves.

Halloween postcard, c.1900

THANKSGIVING MINCEMEAT CAKE

½ cup butter or margarine, softened
1 cup sugar
2 eggs
1 teaspoon baking soda
1 cup buttermilk
2 cups all-purpose flour
1 (9-ounce) package condensed mincemeat, crumbled
Caramel Cream Frosting

Cream butter in a large mixing bowl; gradually add sugar, beating well. Add eggs, one at a time, beating mixture well after each addition.

Dissolve soda in buttermilk, stirring well. Add flour to creamed mixture alternately with buttermilk mixture, beginning and ending with flour. Mix well after each addition. Stir in crumbled mincemeat.

Spoon batter into 2 greased and floured 8-inch round cakepans. Bake at 300° for 45 to 50 minutes or until a wooden pick inserted in center comes out clean. Cool in pans 10 minutes; remove layers from pans, and let cool completely.

Spread Caramel Cream Frosting between layers and on top and sides of cake. Yield: one 2-layer cake.

Caramel Cream Frosting:

1 cup plus 2 tablespoons sugar, divided
½ cup butter or margarine
½ cup whipping cream

Place 2 tablespoons sugar in a saucepan; cook over medium heat until sugar is dissolved and becomes golden brown in color. Set aside.

Combine remaining 1 cup sugar, butter, and cream in a medium saucepan; cook over medium heat, stirring constantly, until mixture comes to a boil. Stir in caramelized sugar. Return to a boil; cook 2 minutes, stirring constantly. Remove from heat; beat until spreading consistency. Yield: enough for one 2-layer cake.

HAPPY BIRTHDAY!

COCONUT BIRTHDAY CAKE

⅓ cup shortening
⅓ cup butter, softened
1¾ cups sugar
3 cups cake flour
3½ teaspoons baking powder
¾ teaspoon salt
1⅓ cups milk
2 teaspoons vanilla extract
4 egg whites
Lemon Filling
Fluffy Frosting
Freshly grated coconut

Cream shortening and butter; gradually add sugar, beating mixture well.

Sift together flour, baking powder, and salt; add to creamed mixture alternately with milk, beating well after each addition. Stir in vanilla.

Beat egg whites (at room temperature) until stiff peaks form; fold into batter.

Pour batter into 3 greased and floured 9-inch round cakepans; bake at 350° for 20 to 25 minutes or until a wooden pick inserted in center comes out clean. Cool in pans 10 minutes; remove layers from pans, and let cool completely. Spread Lemon Filling between layers; frost top and sides with Fluffy Frosting, and sprinkle with coconut. Yield: one 3-layer cake.

Coconut Birthday Cake: filled with lemon flavor

Lemon Filling:

1 cup plus 2 tablespoons sugar
¼ cup cornstarch
1 cup plus 2 tablespoons water
2 egg yolks, slightly beaten
2 tablespoons butter
1 tablespoon grated lemon rind
3 tablespoons lemon juice

Combine sugar and cornstarch; gradually stir in water. Cook over medium heat, stirring constantly, until mixture thickens and boils. Continue boiling 1 minute.

Gradually stir one-fourth of hot mixture into egg yolks; add to remaining hot mixture, stirring constantly. Return to a boil; cook 1 to 2 minutes longer, stirring constantly. Remove from heat and continue stirring until smooth. Stir in butter, lemon rind, and lemon juice. Cool. Yield: about 2 cups.

Fluffy Frosting:

1 cup sugar
⅓ cup water
¼ teaspoon cream of tartar
2 egg whites
½ teaspoon vanilla extract
½ teaspoon almond extract

Combine sugar, water, and cream of tartar in a heavy saucepan. Cook over medium heat, without stirring, until mixture reaches thread stage (232°).

Beat egg whites (at room temperature) until soft peaks form; continue to beat, slowly adding syrup mixture. Add flavorings; beat well. Yield: enough for one 3-layer cake.

MISS ARINTHA'S BIRTHDAY CAKE

¾ cup butter, softened
2 cups sugar
4 eggs, separated
2½ cups all-purpose flour
2 teaspoons baking powder
¼ teaspoon salt
1 cup milk
2 teaspoons vanilla extract
Frosting (recipe follows)
Pecan halves

Cream butter; gradually add sugar, beating well. Add egg yolks, one at a time, beating well after each addition.

Combine flour, baking powder, and salt; add to creamed mixture alternately with milk, beginning and ending with flour mixture. Mix well after each addition. Stir in vanilla.

Beat egg whites (at room temperature) until stiff peaks form. Gently fold into batter.

Pour batter into 2 greased and floured 9-inch round cakepans. Bake at 325° for 40 to 45 minutes or until a wooden pick inserted in center comes out clean. Cool in pans 10 minutes; remove layers from pans, and let cool completely.

Spread frosting between layers and on top and sides of cake. Garnish with pecan halves. Yield: one 2-layer cake.

Frosting:

¾ cup butter or margarine
3 (1-ounce) squares
  semisweet chocolate
¾ cup milk
2¼ cups sugar
1½ tablespoons corn syrup
1½ teaspoons vanilla extract

Combine butter and chocolate in a heavy saucepan; cook over low heat until chocolate melts. Add milk, sugar, and syrup; bring mixture to a boil, and cook 2½ minutes.

Remove from heat, and cool 5 minutes. Add vanilla; stir well. Beat on high speed of electric mixer for 10 minutes or until mixture reaches spreading consistency. Yield: enough for one (9-inch) 2-layer cake.

Valentine Museum. Richmond. Virginia

Decorative illustration from Dennison's *Party Magazine, 1927*

MOTHER ANN'S BIRTHDAY CAKE

1 cup butter or margarine, softened
2 cups sugar
3 cups all-purpose flour
¼ cup cornstarch
1 tablespoon baking powder
½ teaspoon salt
1 cup milk
2 teaspoons vanilla extract
12 egg whites
About 1 cup peach jam
Butter Cream Frosting

Cream butter; gradually add sugar, beating well.

Combine flour, cornstarch, baking powder, and salt; add to creamed mixture alternately with milk, beginning and ending with flour mixture. Mix well after each addition. Stir in the vanilla.

Beat egg whites (at room temperature) until stiff peaks form; fold into batter.

Spoon batter into 3 greased and floured 9-inch round cakepans. Bake at 350° for 25 to 30 minutes or until a wooden pick inserted in center comes out clean. Cool in pans 10 minutes; remove layers from pans, and let cool completely.

Spread peach jam between layers; spread top and sides with Butter Cream Frosting. Yield: one 3-layer cake.

Butter Cream Frosting:

¾ cup butter or margarine, softened
2¼ cups sifted powdered sugar
3 tablespoons milk
¾ teaspoon vanilla extract

Cream butter; gradually add sugar, beating well. Add milk and vanilla, beating until smooth. Yield: enough for one 3-layer cake.

Birthday party captured by first home movie camera, 1923

Ann Lee, born in England in 1736, not only founded the Shaker movement in America but also had a cake named for her. To commemorate her birthday each year, the Shakers served Mother Ann's special cake. The original recipe should be taken seriously, as the Shakers did not indulge in frivolity: "Cut a handful of peach twigs which are filled with sap at this season of the year. Clip the ends and bruise them, and beat the cake batter with them. This will impart a delicate peach flavor to the cake." The recipe obviously pre-dates the rotary beater.

The Heritage Wedding Cake
is romantic with ribbons
and fresh flowers.

Bridal party favor: A small box covered with white crepe paper, decorated with orange blossoms and satin ribbons. From a novelties catalogue, c.1909. We use plainer boxes now for the guests to take home leftover pieces of wedding cake.

Until well into the present century, especially in the rural South, guests would "honor" the bridal couple with a charivari, a custom dating back to frontier days. It is pronounced "shivaree" and derives from the Latin word for headache. The point was to create an awful din outside the bridal chamber and to keep it up all night.

HERITAGE WEDDING CAKE

1½ cups shortening
3 cups sugar
4½ cups all-purpose flour
1 tablespoon baking powder
½ teaspoon salt
1½ cups cold water
2¼ teaspoons imitation
  butter flavor
1½ teaspoons almond
  extract
9 egg whites
Apricot Filling
Ornamental Frosting

Cream shortening in large mixing bowl; gradually add sugar, beating well. Sift dry ingredients together; add to creamed mixture alternately with cold water beginning and ending with flour mixture. Mix well after each addition. Stir in flavorings and beat well.

Beat egg whites (at room temperature) until soft peaks form; fold into batter. Pour batter into 1 greased and floured 13- x 9- x 2-inch pan and 1 greased and floured 7½- x 3- x 2-inch loafpan. Bake at 325° for 1 hour and 10 minutes or until a wooden pick inserted in center comes out clean. Cool in pans 10 minutes; remove from pans, and let cool completely on wire racks.

Slice each layer in half horizontally; spread Apricot Filling between sliced layers, placing larger layer, bottom side down, on cake plate. Spread top and sides of bottom layer with Ornamental Frosting. Place smaller layer, bottom side down, in middle of larger layer. Spread top and sides of top layer with Ornamental Frosting. Decorate cake using decorating bags and tips with remaining Ornamental Frosting. Yield: one 13- x 9-inch layer cake.

Apricot Filling:

1 (8¾-ounce) can apricot
  halves, drained
¼ cup Grand Marnier or
  other orange-flavored
  liqueur, optional

Combine apricots and liqueur in container of electric blender. Blend well. Yield: about 1 cup.

Ornamental Frosting:

1½ cups shortening
3 (16-ounce) packages
  powdered sugar, sifted and
  divided
1 egg white
¾ teaspoon salt
1½ teaspoons vanilla
  extract
½ to ¾ cup whipping cream,
  lukewarm

Cream shortening in large mixing bowl using medium speed of an electric mixer; gradually add half of sugar. Cream until light and fluffy.

Add egg white (at room temperature), salt, and vanilla; mix well. Add remaining sugar and ½ cup whipping cream alternately, beginning and ending with sugar; add more whipping cream if necessary. Mix well after each addition. Continue beating until the mixture is fluffy and creamy. Yield: about 4½ cups.

Note: Frosting will keep in an airtight container in the refrigerator for several days.

BRIDE'S CAKE

1½ cups butter or margarine,
  softened
3 cups sugar
4½ cups sifted all-purpose
  flour
¾ teaspoon baking soda
¾ cup milk
1 teaspoon almond extract
1 teaspoon vanilla extract
12 egg whites
1 teaspoon cream of tartar
Ornamental Icing

Cream butter; gradually add sugar, beating well.

Combine flour and soda; sift 3 times. Add to creamed mixture alternately with milk, beginning and ending with flour mixture. Mix well after each addition (the mixture will be stiff). Stir in flavorings.

Beat egg whites (at room temperature) until frothy; add cream of tartar, and beat until stiff peaks form. Fold into creamed mixture.

Pour batter into a greased and floured 10-inch tube pan. Bake at 325° for 1 hour and 30 minutes or until cake tests done. Cool in pan 10 to 15 minutes; remove from pan, and let cool completely. Spread top and sides of cake with Ornamental Icing. Yield: one 10-inch cake.

Ornamental Icing:

1 cup shortening
2 (16-ounce) packages
  powdered sugar, sifted
  and divided
1 egg white
½ teaspoon salt
½ cup half-and-half
1 teaspoon vanilla
  extract

Combine shortening and one package of sugar; beat well. Add remaining ingredients, beating until smooth. Yield: enough for one 10-inch cake.

Note: Icing may be stored in an airtight container in refrigerator for several days.

Tin ornamenting tubes

Stereograph of a wedding celebration, late 19th century

CHOCOLATE GROOM'S CAKE

1 cup butter or margarine, softened
2 cups sugar
5 eggs
1 teaspoon baking soda
1 cup buttermilk
2¼ cups sifted cake flour
3 (1-ounce) squares unsweetened chocolate, melted
1 teaspoon vanilla extract
Special Chocolate Frosting

Cream butter; gradually add sugar, beating well. Add eggs, one at a time, beating well after each addition.

Dissolve soda in buttermilk; add to creamed mixture alternately with flour, beginning and ending with flour. Mix well after each addition. Add chocolate; mix well. Stir in vanilla.

Pour batter into a greased and floured 10-inch tube pan. Bake at 350° for 1 hour or until cake tests done. Cool in pan 10 to 15 minutes; remove from pan, and let cool completely.

Spread Special Chocolate Frosting on top and sides of cake. Yield: one 10-inch cake.

Special Chocolate Frosting:

½ cup butter or margarine, softened
1 egg yolk
1 cup cocoa
4½ cups sifted powdered sugar
¼ cup milk
1 teaspoon vanilla extract

Cream butter; add egg yolk and cocoa, beating well. Add sugar alternately with milk, beating until smooth enough to spread. Stir in vanilla. Yield: enough for one 10-inch cake.

TRADITIONAL WEDDING FRUITCAKE

2 (15-ounce) packages raisins, chopped
1 (10-ounce) package currants
3 (4-ounce) packages chopped candied citron
1 (16-ounce) package candied pineapple slices, chopped
1 (8-ounce) package candied red cherries, chopped
1 tablespoon chopped candied orange peel
1 tablespoon chopped candied lemon peel
3½ cups chopped pecans
2 cups all-purpose flour, divided
1 cup butter or margarine, softened
1 cup brown sugar, firmly packed
6 eggs
¼ cup molasses
2 tablespoons cocoa
1 teaspoon baking powder
½ teaspoon baking soda
½ teaspoon salt
2 teaspoons ground allspice
2 teaspoons ground nutmeg
2 teaspoons ground cinnamon
2 teaspoons ground cloves
½ cup buttermilk
½ cup red wine

Combine first 8 ingredients; dredge with ¾ cup flour, stirring to coat well. Set aside.

Cream butter in a large mixing bowl; gradually add sugar, beating until light and fluffy. Add eggs, one at a time, beating well after each addition. Stir in molasses.

Combine remaining 1¼ cups flour, cocoa, baking powder, soda, salt, and spices; add to creamed mixture alternately with buttermilk and wine, mixing well after each addition. Stir in dredged fruit.

Spoon batter into a greased and floured 10-inch tube pan. Bake at 275° for 3½ to 4 hours or until cake tests done. Cool cake completely in pan. Yield: one 10-inch cake.

PETITS FOURS

½ cup plus 1 tablespoon butter or margarine, softened
1¼ cups sugar
3 eggs
2 cups all-purpose flour
1 tablespoon baking powder
½ teaspoon salt
¾ cup milk
Simple Syrup
Strawberry jam
Frosting (recipe follows)

Grease a 13- x 9- x 2-inch baking pan heavily with butter; set aside.

Cream butter; gradually add sugar, beating well. Add eggs, one at a time, beating well after each addition.

Combine flour, baking powder, and salt; add to creamed mixture alternately with milk, beginning and ending with flour mixture.

Pour batter into prepared pan and bake at 375° for 25 to 30 minutes or until a wooden pick inserted in center comes out clean. Cool in pan 10 minutes; remove from pan and allow to cool on wire racks.

Wrap cake tightly in foil; freeze for several hours or until firm. Slice cake horizontally and brush layers with Simple Syrup; spread strawberry jam on lower layer, and replace with top layer (layers will be thin).

Cut cake in 2-inch squares. Place squares two inches apart on a wire rack; place rack in a large shallow pan. Quickly pour the warm frosting over cakes, completely covering top and sides. Spoon up all frosting that drips through the rack, and reheat to pouring consistency; add a small amount of water, if necessary, to maintain original consistency. Continue pouring and reheating until all cakes are frosted. Allow frosting to dry.

Place cakes on a cutting board; using a sharp knife, trim any surplus frosting from the bottom of each cake. Yield: 2 dozen.

Simple Syrup:

1 cup sugar
1 cup water
1 tablespoon brandy

Combine sugar and water in a medium saucepan. Bring to a boil, and simmer 10 minutes. Remove syrup from heat and add brandy. Cool. Yield: about 1 cup.

Frosting:

6 cups sifted powdered sugar
¼ cup plus 1 tablespoon water
¼ cup plus 1 tablespoon light corn syrup
1 teaspoon vanilla extract
Food coloring

Combine first 4 ingredients in top of a double boiler. Place over boiling water, stirring until sugar is melted and mixture is smooth and glossy. Add food coloring to obtain desired color. Yield: about 4 cups.

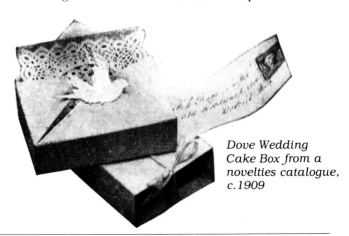

Dove Wedding Cake Box from a novelties catalogue, c.1909

BACK TO BASICS

For a practical overview of the cake family, we may conveniently divide it into five categories (not counting fruitcakes, which are a law unto themselves). Southerners are on a first-name basis with them all: Pound, Sponge, Layer, Angel, and Chiffon. Interestingly, all but two are American developments.

The pound cake is undeniably British, certainly not new when it appeared in Hannah Glasse's *The Art of Cookery Made Plain and Easy*, published in England in 1747.

The sponge cake's lineage can be traced back from Mary Randolph's "Savoy or Spunge Cake," which appeared in her *The Virginia Housewife or Methodical Cook* in 1824, to the French "Savoi." One could infer another step back in time: Early writers include a form of sponge cakes called Naples biscuits, which we know as ladyfingers.

With the European pound cake as a point of departure, experimental bakers found that some of the pound cake's butter and eggs could be replaced by liquid, so long as baking powder was there to counteract the tendency of liquid to tighten the batter. Eggs could now be used whole; no need to rely solely on whipped egg whites for leavening. Flavoring depended on the cook's ingenuity; vanilla was there, thanks to Thomas Jefferson, and chocolate. An exotic way to flavor a cake batter turns up in a version of a basic pound cake. Its rich taste can be further "improved," depending on one's taste, by lining the pan with fresh rose geranium leaves.

The South's role in the evolution of the layer cake from the pound cake is well defined by the names we have given them; Robert E. Lee, Lane, Williamsburg, to name a few. It was baking powder that helped most to bring Southern layer cakes to perfection.

The angel food cake's origins are obscure. We may take or leave this apocryphal story: A woman on the east coast was given the recipe by a visitor who claimed it had originated in India. The happy donee baked the cake behind closed doors in her commercial bakery for a time, but the secret leaked out, as secrets do. Southerners prefer to think of a frugal ancestress casting a beady eye on egg whites left from a pound cake and doing something creative about them.

The chiffon cake is the youngest of the family, from 1927, and the only one that flaunts a birth certificate.

From back to front: Chocolate Chiffon Cake (page 114), ready for whipped cream frosting. Lemon Roll (page 127), rolled and cooled, awaits Tart Lemon Filling. White Layer Cake (page 117) cools ten minutes in pans.

ANGEL FOOD CAKES

BASIC ANGEL FOOD CAKE

12 egg whites
1 teaspoon cream of tartar
Pinch of salt
1 teaspoon water
1½ cups sugar
1 cup sifted cake flour
1 teaspoon vanilla extract
½ teaspoon almond
  extract

Beat egg whites (at room temperature) until foamy. Add cream of tartar, salt, and water; beat until soft peaks form. Add sugar, 2 tablespoons at a time, beating until stiff peaks form. Sprinkle flour over egg white mixture, ¼ cup at a time; fold in carefully. Fold in flavorings.

Pour batter into an ungreased 10-inch tube pan, spreading evenly with a spatula. Bake at 325° for 45 minutes or until cake springs back when lightly touched. Remove from oven, and invert pan. Cool 40 minutes; remove cake from pan. Yield: one 10-inch cake.

Pineapple Angel Food Cake:

1¼ cups sifted powdered
  sugar
2 tablespoons butter, softened
1 egg yolk, beaten
2 tablespoons pineapple juice
1 teaspoon grated lemon rind
3 tablespoons crushed
  pineapple

Combine all ingredients, except pineapple; beat at medium speed of an electric mixer about 2 minutes or until slightly thickened. Stir in pineapple. Spoon Pineapple Glaze over cake. Yield: about 1 cup.

Lemon Angel Food Cake:

For a lemon-flavored cake, substitute ½ teaspoon lemon extract for almond extract.

Chocolate Angel Food Cake:

For a chocolate cake variation, add ¼ cup sifted cocoa to cake flour; do not glaze.

Basic Angel Food Cake (top) and squares of Self-Frosting Angel Cake (below)

SELF-FROSTING ANGEL CAKE

6 egg whites
½ teaspoon cream of tartar
⅛ teaspoon salt
¼ cup plus 2 tablespoons
  sugar
½ cup sifted cake flour
½ teaspoon vanilla extract
⅛ teaspoon almond
  extract
½ cup flaked coconut

Beat egg whites (at room temperature) until foamy; add cream of tartar and salt; beat until soft peaks form. Gradually add sugar, 2 tablespoons at a time, beating mixture until stiff peaks form.

Sprinkle flour over egg white mixture; fold in carefully. Gently fold in flavorings.

Pour batter into an ungreased 9-inch square baking pan; sprinkle coconut over top. Bake at 325° for 30 minutes or until a wooden pick inserted in center comes out clean. Cool in pan about 40 minutes. Remove cake from pan, and cut into squares to serve. Yield: one 9-inch cake.

COFFEE ANGEL FOOD CAKE

1½ cups sugar, divided
1 cup sifted cake flour
10 egg whites
½ teaspoon salt
1¼ teaspoons cream of
tartar
1 tablespoon instant coffee
powder
½ teaspoon vanilla extract
Butter Cream Frosting
Slivered almonds (optional)

Combine ½ cup sugar and flour; set aside.

Beat egg whites (at room temperature) until foamy; add salt. Beat until soft peaks form. Add cream of tartar; continue beating until peaks are stiff and glossy. Gradually fold in remaining 1 cup sugar. Sprinkle about one-fourth of flour mixture over whites; fold in carefully. Repeat procedure with remaining flour mixture, using one-fourth at a time. Fold in the coffee powder and vanilla.

Pour batter into an ungreased 10-inch tube pan, spreading evenly with a spatula. Bake at 350° for 35 to 40 minutes or until cake springs back when lightly touched. Remove from oven, and invert pan. Cool 40 minutes, and remove cake from pan. Spread Butter Cream Frosting over top of cooled cake and sprinkle with slivered almonds, if desired. Yield: one 10-inch cake.

Butter Cream Frosting:

⅔ cup butter or margarine,
softened
3 cups sifted powdered
sugar
1 tablespoon whipping cream
2 teaspoons instant coffee
powder
1 teaspoon vanilla extract

Combine butter and sugar, beating well with electric mixer. Dissolve coffee powder in whipping cream, stirring well. Add to creamed mixture, beating until smooth enough to spread. Add vanilla, and beat well. Yield: enough for one 10-inch cake.

MOCK ANGEL FOOD CAKE

2 cups cake flour
1½ cups sugar
2 teaspoons baking powder
1 cup milk, scalded
4 egg whites
Pineapple Topping

Sift flour, sugar, and baking powder together 3 times. Pour hot milk slowly into flour mixture, beating constantly.

Beat egg whites (at room temperature) until soft peaks form. Gently fold into batter.

Pour batter into 2 ungreased 9-inch round cakepans. Bake at 350° for 25 minutes or until cake springs back when lightly touched. Cool in pans about 40 minutes.

Remove layers from pans, and spread Pineapple Topping between layers and on top and sides of cooled cake. Yield: one 2-layer cake.

Pineapple Topping:

1 cup sugar
2½ tablespoons all-purpose
flour
1¼ cups milk
4 egg yolks
½ cup crushed pineapple,
well drained

Combine sugar and flour in top of double boiler; gradually stir in milk. Cook over medium heat about 5 minutes, stirring constantly until thickened.

Beat egg yolks until thick and lemon colored. Gradually stir about ¼ of hot mixture into yolks; add to remaining hot mixture, stirring constantly. Cook over medium heat, stirring constantly, about 2 minutes or until thickened. Remove from heat, and stir in pineapple. Let cool. Yield: about 2½ cups.

19th-century advertisement

THE EGG

CHIFFON CAKES

T he youngest cake by far in the Southern lexicon is the chiffon. Richer than angel cake, but almost as light, it is the only one we can truly call an invention and put a date on the event. Californian Henry Baker originated the chiffon cake in 1927 and for twenty years it remained his "little secret."

Eventually Baker sold his formula to General Mills with the result that, in the late 1940s, chiffon cake hit an enthusiastic market. The surprise ingredient was, of course, salad oil.

Chiffon cake variations are legion because it is easy to make and takes well to practically any flavoring agent, from chocolate to citrus to liqueurs.

CHOCOLATE CHIFFON

1½ cups sifted cake flour
2¼ cups sugar, divided
⅔ cup sifted cocoa
1 teaspoon baking soda
½ teaspoon salt
¼ cup plus 3 tablespoons
   vegetable oil
8 eggs, separated
¾ cup water
1 teaspoon vanilla extract
1 cup whipping cream
¼ cup sifted powdered
   sugar
Chopped walnuts (optional)

Sift together flour, 1¾ cups sugar, cocoa, soda, and salt in a large mixing bowl. Make a well in center of dry ingredients; add oil, egg yolks, water, and vanilla. Beat at high speed of electric mixer 5 minutes or until mixture is smooth.

Beat egg whites (at room temperature) in a large mixing bowl at medium speed of electric mixer until soft peaks form. Add remaining ½ cup sugar, 2 tablespoons at a time, and beat about 4 minutes at medium speed or until stiff peaks form.

Pour egg yolk mixture in a thin, steady stream over entire surface of egg whites. Gently fold the chocolate-yolk mixture into whites.

Pour batter into an ungreased 10-inch tube pan, spreading evenly with a spatula. Bake at 350° for 1 hour or until cake springs back when lightly touched. Remove from oven; invert pan, and let cool completely before removing cake from pan.

Beat whipping cream until foamy; gradually add powdered sugar, beating until soft peaks form. Frost top of cake with whipped cream, and garnish with walnuts, if desired. Yield: one 10-inch cake.

Hershey Foods Corporation

Employee working at a labeling machine on Hershey's Cocoa can line, early 1920s

LEMON GOLD CAKE

2½ cups all-purpose flour
1½ cups sugar, divided
1 tablespoon baking powder
1 teaspoon salt
½ cup vegetable oil
6 eggs, separated
¾ cup water
1 teaspoon grated lemon rind
2 teaspoons lemon juice
½ teaspoon cream of tartar
Lemon Fluffy Frosting

Sift together flour, 1 cup sugar, baking powder, and salt in a small mixing bowl. Make a well in center of dry ingredients; add oil, egg yolks, water, lemon rind, and juice. Beat at high speed of electric mixer 5 minutes or until smooth.

Combine egg whites (at room temperature) and cream of tartar in a large mixing bowl; beat at medium speed of electric mixer until soft peaks form. Add remaining ½ cup sugar, 2 tablespoons at a time, and beat about 4 minutes at medium speed or until stiff peaks form.

Pour egg yolk mixture in a thin, steady stream over entire surface of egg whites; gently fold yolk mixture into whites.

Pour batter into an ungreased 10-inch tube pan, spreading evenly with a spatula. Bake at 325° for 55 to 60 minutes or until cake tests done. Remove from oven; invert pan, and let cool completely. Remove from pan, and spread Lemon Fluffy Frosting over top. Yield: one 10-inch cake.

Lemon Fluffy Frosting:

½ cup butter or margarine, softened
4 cups sifted powdered sugar, divided
2 teaspoons grated lemon rind
3 tablespoons lemon juice
Dash of salt

Combine butter and 2 cups powdered sugar, beating well. Gradually add remaining ingredients; beat until smooth. Yield: enough for one 10-inch cake.

Praline Chiffon Cake is aromatic with maple.

PRALINE CHIFFON CAKE

2 cups sifted all-purpose flour
¾ cup sugar
¾ cup firmly packed brown sugar
1 tablespoon baking powder
½ teaspoon salt
½ cup vegetable oil
7 eggs, separated
¾ cup cold water
2 teaspoons maple flavoring
1 teaspoon cream of tartar

Combine dry ingredients in a medium mixing bowl. Make a well in center; add oil, egg yolks, water, and flavoring. Stir just until moistened.

Beat egg whites (at room temperature) in a large mixing bowl until foamy; add cream of tartar, beating until stiff peaks form. Gently fold yolk mixture into egg whites.

Pour batter into an ungreased 10-inch tube pan, spreading evenly with spatula. Bake at 325° for 1 hour and 10 minutes or until cake springs back when lightly touched. Remove from oven, and invert pan. Cool 40 minutes, and remove cake from pan. Yield: one 10-inch cake.

An afternoon get-together complete with cake and ice cream.

BASIC YELLOW CAKE

1 cup butter or margarine,
  softened
2 cups sugar
5 eggs
3 cups sifted all-purpose
  flour
1 tablespoon baking
  powder
1¼ cups milk
1 teaspoon vanilla extract

Cream butter; gradually add sugar, beating well. Add eggs, one at a time, beating well after each addition.

Combine flour and baking powder; add to creamed mixture alternately with milk, beginning and ending with flour mixture. Stir in vanilla.

Pour batter into 2 greased and floured 9-inch round cakepans. Bake at 350° for 25 minutes or until a wooden pick inserted in center comes out clean. Cool in pans 10 minutes; remove layers from pans, and cool completely. Yield: one 2-layer cake.

Spice Cake:

For a spice cake variation, add ½ teaspoon ground nutmeg, ½ teaspoon ground cinnamon, ½ teaspoon ground cloves, and ½ teaspoon ground allspice to flour mixture.

Chocolate Cake:

For a simple chocolate cake, add three (1-ounce) squares unsweetened chocolate, melted, to creamed mixture.

WHITE LAYER CAKE

½ cup shortening
1¼ cups sugar
2 cups all-purpose flour
2½ teaspoons baking powder
½ teaspoon salt
¾ cup milk
1 teaspoon vanilla extract
3 egg whites

Cream shortening; gradually add sugar, beating well.

Combine flour, baking powder, and salt; add to creamed mixture alternately with milk, beginning and ending with flour mixture. Stir in vanilla.

Beat egg whites (at room temperature) until stiff peaks form; fold into batter.

Pour batter into 2 greased and floured 8-inch round or square cakepans. Bake at 350° for 25 minutes or until a wooden pick inserted in center comes out clean. Cool in pans 10 minutes; remove layers from pans, and let cool completely. Yield: one 2-layer cake.

SILVER CAKE

½ cup butter or margarine, softened
1½ cups sugar
3 cups all-purpose flour
1 tablespoon baking powder
1 cup milk
½ teaspoon lemon extract
4 egg whites

Cream butter; gradually add sugar, beating well.

Combine flour and baking powder; add to creamed mixture alternately with milk, beginning and ending with flour mixture. Mix well after each addition. Stir in lemon extract.

Beat egg whites (at room temperature) until stiff but not dry; gently fold into batter.

Pour batter into 2 greased and floured 9-inch round cakepans. Bake at 375° for 25 to 30 minutes or until a wooden pick inserted in center comes out clean. Cool in pans 10 minutes; remove layers from pans, and let cool completely. Yield: one 2-layer cake.

DEVIL'S FOOD CAKE

½ cup butter or margarine, softened
1½ cups sugar
2 eggs
½ cup hot water
2 cups all-purpose flour
½ cup cocoa
½ teaspoon baking soda
½ teaspoon salt
½ cup milk
1 teaspoon vanilla

Cream butter in a large mixing bowl; add sugar, beating well. Add eggs, one at a time, beating well after each addition. Add water; beat well.

Combine flour, cocoa, soda, and salt; add to creamed mixture alternately with milk, beginning and ending with flour mixture. Mix well after each addition. Stir in vanilla.

Pour batter into 2 greased and floured 9-inch round cakepans. Bake at 350° for 25 minutes or until a wooden pick inserted in center comes out clean. Cool in pans 10 minutes; remove layers from pans, and let cool completely. Yield: one 2-layer cake.

1-2-3-4 CAKE

1 cup butter or margarine, softened
2 cups sugar
4 eggs, separated
3 cups all-purpose flour
1 tablespoon baking powder
½ teaspoon salt
1 cup milk
1 teaspoon vanilla extract

Cream butter; gradually add sugar, beating well. Add egg yolks, beating well.

Combine flour, baking powder, and salt; add to creamed mixture alternately with milk, beginning and ending with flour mixture. Mix well after each addition. Stir in vanilla.

Beat egg whites (at room temperature) until stiff peaks form; fold into batter.

Pour batter into 3 greased and floured 9-inch round cakepans. Bake at 350° for 25 minutes or until a wooden pick inserted in center comes out clean. Cool in pans 10 minutes; remove layers from pans, and let cool completely. Yield: one 3-layer cake.

Flour sifter

After the Civil War, when mass production of kitchen labor-savers became possible, Southern cooks who could afford them eagerly collected everything from coffee roasters and grinders to the latest in flour sifters. But even after she had traded in her wood-burning cookstove for a new gas range in the 1920s and 30s, the home baker was still doing her best to test-guess her oven temperature, waiting, as had the writer back in 1886, for the day "when some enterprising 'Dixie' Girl shall invent a stove or range with a thermometer attached to the oven, so that the heat may be regulated accurately and intelligently."

POUND CAKES

APPLE CIDER POUND CAKE

1 cup butter or margarine,
  softened
½ cup shortening
3 cups sugar
6 eggs
3 cups all-purpose flour
½ teaspoon baking powder
½ teaspoon salt
¾ teaspoon ground cinnamon
½ teaspoon ground allspice
½ teaspoon ground nutmeg
¼ teaspoon ground cloves
1 cup apple cider
1 teaspoon vanilla extract

Combine butter and shortening, mixing well; gradually add sugar, beating well. Add eggs, one at a time, beating well after each addition.

Combine dry ingredients; add to creamed mixture alternately with apple cider, beginning and ending with flour mixture. Mix well after each addition. Stir in vanilla.

Pour batter into a well-greased 10-inch tube pan. Bake at 325° for 1 hour and 50 minutes or until cake tests done. Cool in pan 10 to 15 minutes; remove cake from pan, and let cool completely. Yield: one 10-inch cake.

When Mary Randolph wrote the preface to her *The Virginia Housewife or Methodical Cook* in 1824, she declared her recipes were "written from memory, where they were impressed by long continued practice." Her work, generally regarded as the first "Southern" cookbook, is an early hybrid, containing a fascinating American-English melange of recipes from Indian Meal Pudding to Plum Pudding. The pound cake is there, testimony to Mrs. Randolph's English heritage.

TEXAS BRANDY POUND CAKE

2 cups butter, softened
2 cups sugar
9 eggs
4 cups all-purpose flour
½ teaspoon cream of
  tartar
½ teaspoon salt
2 tablespoons brandy

Cream butter; gradually add sugar, beating well. Add eggs, one at a time, beating well after each addition.

Combine the flour, cream of tartar, and salt; add to creamed mixture, mixing well. Stir in the brandy.

Pour batter into 2 well-greased 9- x 5- x 3-inch loafpans. Bake at 325° for 1 hour and 10 minutes or until a wooden pick inserted in center comes out clean. Cool in pans 10 minutes; remove from pans, and let cool completely. Yield: 2 loaves.

GERANIUM POUND CAKE

The name of this cake is derived from the rose geranium leaves (*Pelargonium graveolens*) that may be used to line the pan before pouring in the batter. The addition of geranium adds a strong "rose geranium" taste to the finished cake.

1 cup butter or margarine,
  softened
2 cups sugar
3 eggs
3 cups all-purpose flour
2 teaspoons baking powder
1 cup milk
1 teaspoon vanilla extract
Rose geranium leaves
  (optional)
Powdered sugar (optional)

Cream butter; gradually add sugar, beating well. Add eggs, one at a time, beating well after each addition. Combine flour and baking powder; add to creamed mixture alternately with milk, beginning and ending with flour mixture. Stir in the vanilla.

Line a well-greased 10-inch tube pan with the geranium leaves, if desired; pour batter into pan. Bake at 350° for 1 hour or until cake tests done. Cool in pan 15 minutes; remove from pan, and let cool completely. Sift powdered sugar over top of cake, if desired. Yield: one 10-inch cake.

PECAN-TOPPED CHOCOLATE POUND CAKE

1 cup butter or margarine,
  softened
½ cup shortening
2½ cups sugar
5 eggs
3 cups all-purpose flour
½ cup cocoa
1 cup milk
1 cup chopped pecans

Combine butter and shortening, mixing well; gradually add sugar, beating until light and fluffy. Add eggs, one at a time, beating well after each addition. Combine flour and cocoa; add to creamed mixture alternately with milk, beginning and ending with flour mixture. Mix well after each addition.

Pour batter into a well-greased 10-inch tube pan. Sprinkle pecans evenly over batter. Bake at 325° for 1 hour and 15 minutes or until cake tests done. Cool in pan 15 minutes; remove from pan, and let cake cool completely. Yield: one 10-inch cake.

Texas Brandy Pound Cake (top), Geranium Pound Cake (center), and Pecan-Topped Chocolate Pound Cake (below). These adaptations of old English pound cake would make a star-studded dessert buffet party.

Cream Cheese Pound Cake: no need to frost a cake so rich

CREAM CHEESE POUND CAKE

1 cup margarine, softened
½ cup butter, softened (do not substitute)
1 (8-ounce) package cream cheese, softened
3 cups sugar
6 eggs
3 cups sifted cake flour
2 teaspoons vanilla extract

Combine first 3 ingredients; beat well with a heavy-duty mixer. Gradually add sugar; beat until light and fluffy (about 5 minutes). Add eggs, one at a time; beat well after each addition. Add flour to creamed mixture; beat well. Stir in vanilla.

Pour batter into a well-greased 10-inch tube pan. Bake at 325° for 1 hour and 30 minutes or until cake tests done. Cool in pan 10 minutes; remove from pan, and cool completely. Yield: one 10-inch cake.

BROWN SUGAR POUND CAKE

1 cup shortening
½ cup butter or margarine, softened
1 (16-ounce) package brown sugar
5 eggs
3 cups all-purpose flour
½ teaspoon salt
½ teaspoon baking powder
1 cup evaporated milk
2 teaspoons maple flavoring
Brown Sugar Frosting

Combine shortening and butter in a large mixing bowl; mix well. Gradually add sugar, beating until light and fluffy. Add eggs, one at a time, beating well after each addition.

Combine flour, salt, and baking powder; add to creamed mixture alternately with milk, beginning and ending with flour mixture. Mix well after each addition. Stir in flavoring.

Pour batter into a well-greased 10-inch tube pan. Bake at 325° for 1 hour and 20 minutes or until cake tests done. Cool in pan 10 to 15 minutes; remove from pan, and cool completely. Spread Brown Sugar Frosting over top of cake. Yield: one 10-inch cake.

Brown Sugar Frosting:

¼ cup butter or margarine
1½ cups sifted powdered sugar
½ cup firmly packed brown sugar
2 tablespoons milk
½ teaspoon vanilla extract

Combine all ingredients in a medium saucepan; cook over low heat, beating until sugar is dissolved and mixture is smooth. Yield: about 1½ cups.

CHOCOLATE POUND CAKE

1 cup shortening
2 cups sugar
4 eggs
½ teaspoon baking soda
1 cup buttermilk
3 cups all-purpose flour
½ teaspoon salt
1 (4-ounce) package sweet
  baking chocolate, melted
2 teaspoons vanilla extract
2 teaspoons butter flavoring

Cream shortening; gradually add sugar, beating well. Add eggs, one at a time, beating well after each addition.

Dissolve soda in buttermilk. Combine flour and salt; add to creamed mixture alternately with buttermilk mixture, beginning and ending with flour mixture. Mix well after each addition. Add chocolate, beating well. Stir in flavorings.

Pour batter into a well-greased 10-inch tube pan. Bake at 325° for 1 hour and 25 minutes or until cake tests done. Cool in pan 15 minutes; remove cake from pan, and let cool completely. Yield: one 10-inch cake.

COCONUT POUND CAKE

1 cup shortening
2 cups sugar
6 eggs
2 cups all-purpose flour
½ teaspoon salt
1½ teaspoons vanilla extract
1 teaspoon butter flavoring
1 (7-ounce) can flaked
  coconut

Cream shortening; gradually add sugar, beating well. Add eggs, one at a time, beating well after each addition. Combine flour and salt; add to creamed mixture, beating well. Stir in flavorings and coconut.

Pour batter into a well-greased 10-inch tube pan. Bake at 325° for 1 hour and 20 minutes or until cake tests done. Cool in pan 10 to 15 minutes; remove from pan, and cool completely. Yield: one 10-inch cake.

MOCHA POUND CAKE

⅔ cup shortening
1¼ cups sugar
3 eggs
2 (1-ounce) squares
  semisweet chocolate, melted
2 to 3 teaspoons instant
  coffee granules
½ cup water
2 cups sifted cake flour
1 teaspoon salt
½ teaspoon cream of tartar
¼ teaspoon baking soda
1 teaspoon vanilla extract

Cream shortening; gradually add sugar, beating until light and fluffy. Add eggs, one at a time, beating well after each addition. Add melted chocolate, mixing well.

Dissolve coffee granules in ½ cup water; stir well, and set aside.

Combine flour, salt, cream of tartar, and soda; gradually add to chocolate mixture alternately with coffee mixture, beginning and ending with flour mixture. Mix well after each addition. Stir in vanilla.

Pour batter into a waxed paper-lined and greased 9- x 5- x 3-inch loafpan. Bake at 325° for 1 hour and 15 minutes or until a wooden pick inserted in center comes out clean. Cool in pan 10 minutes; remove to wire rack, and cool loaf completely. Yield: 1 loaf.

Churning butter

Brown Brothers

SPONGE CAKES

ALMOND SPONGE CAKE

1¼ cups sugar
⅓ cup water
7 eggs, separated
1 teaspoon almond extract
1 cup sifted all-purpose flour

Combine sugar and water in a heavy saucepan. Cook over medium heat, stirring frequently, until mixture comes to a boil and sugar is dissolved. Continue cooking, stirring frequently, until mixture reaches thread stage (234°).

Beat egg whites (at room temperature) until stiff but not dry. While beating at medium speed of electric mixer, pour hot syrup in a thin stream over egg whites. Turn mixer to high, and beat 5 minutes or until cool. Stir in flavoring.

Beat egg yolks until thick and lemon colored; add to whites, and beat well. Sprinkle flour over egg white mixture, ¼ cup at a time; fold well after each addition.

Pour batter into an ungreased 10-inch tube pan, spreading evenly. Bake at 325° for 50 minutes or until cake springs back when lightly touched. Remove from oven; invert pan. Cool 40 minutes; remove from pan. Yield: one 10-inch cake.

Step 1—Cook sugar and water over medium heat, stirring frequently, until mixture reaches thread stage (234°).

Step 4—Beat egg yolks until thick and lemon colored; add to whites, and beat well.

Step 5—Sprinkle sifted flour over egg white mixture, ¼ cup at a time. Fold gently with a down, up and over motion.

Step 2—Beat egg whites (at room temperature) until stiff but not dry.

Step 3—While beating at medium speed of electric mixer, slowly pour hot syrup in a thin stream over egg whites. Beat at high speed 5 minutes or until mixture cools.

Step 6—Rotate bowl frequently while folding in remaining flour. Pour batter into ungreased pan, and place in center of oven rack to ensure even baking.

Step 7—To keep cake from falling or shrinking upon removal from oven, invert pan and cool about 40 minutes. Loosen from sides by sliding a metal spatula around pan.

Delicate Cake

Two cupfuls of white sugar, whites of four eggs, one half cupful of butter. Beat these well together. Add one cupful of milk, two and one half cupfuls of flour, into which one heaping teaspoonful of baking powder has been sifted. Flavor. You may use one cupful of cornstarch in place of the flour. And add half the beaten whites of eggs last.

From Mrs. Mary Wadley's Receipt Book, 1890

DELICATE SPONGE CAKE

1 cup sugar
½ cup water
6 eggs, separated
½ teaspoon vanilla
¼ teaspoon salt
1 cup sifted all-purpose flour

Combine sugar and water in a saucepan. Cook over medium heat, stirring frequently, until mixture comes to a boil and sugar is dissolved. Continue cooking, stirring frequently, until mixture reaches thread stage (234°).

Beat egg whites (at room temperature) until stiff but not dry. While beating at medium speed of electric mixer, slowly pour hot syrup in a thin stream over egg whites. Turn mixer to high speed, and continue beating until mixture is cooled, about 5 minutes.

Combine egg yolks, vanilla, and salt; beat until thick. Add to egg white mixture; beat well. Sprinkle flour over egg white mixture, ¼ cup at a time, folding well after each addition.

Pour batter into an ungreased 10-inch tube pan, spreading evenly with spatula. Bake at 325° for 50 minutes or until cake springs back when lightly touched. Remove from oven, and invert pan. Cool 40 minutes; remove cake from pan. Yield: one 10-inch cake.

Note: Delicate Sponge Cake may also be baked in two 9-inch round cakepans.

GERTRUDE'S CHOCOLATE WHIPPED CREAM ROLL

5 eggs, separated
1 cup sugar, divided
1 teaspoon hot water
¼ cup plus 1 tablespoon
   sifted all-purpose flour
1 teaspoon baking powder
3 tablespoons sifted cocoa
1 cup whipping cream
3 tablespoons sugar
½ teaspoon vanilla extract
Chocolate Frosting
½ cup chopped pecans

Grease a 15- x 10- x 1-inch jelly-roll pan with vegetable oil, and line with waxed paper. Grease waxed paper with vegetable oil; set aside.

Beat egg yolks until thick and lemon colored; gradually add ½ cup sugar, beating constantly. Stir in hot water.

Beat egg whites (at room temperature) until foamy; gradually add remaining ½ cup sugar, beating until stiff but not dry. Fold yolk mixture into whites. Combine flour, baking powder and cocoa; gently fold into egg mixture.

Spread batter evenly in prepared pan. Bake at 400° for 15 minutes or until cake springs back when lightly touched.

Immediately loosen cake from sides of pan, and turn out onto a 15- x 10-inch linen towel. Peel off waxed paper. Starting at narrow end, roll up cake and towel together; cool on a wire rack, seam side down.

Beat whipping cream until foamy; gradually add 3 tablespoons sugar, beating until soft peaks form. Fold in vanilla.

Unroll cake and remove towel. Spread cake with whipped cream; reroll. Place on serving plate, seam side down. Spread Chocolate Frosting on cake; garnish with chopped pecans. Chill. Yield: 8 to 10 servings.

Chocolate Frosting:

4 (1-ounce) squares
   unsweetened chocolate
¼ cup butter or margarine
⅓ cup milk
⅛ teaspoon salt
3 cups sifted powdered sugar
1 teaspoon vanilla extract

Combine first 4 ingredients in top of a double boiler; place over boiling water, stirring constantly, until chocolate and butter are melted. Remove from heat and cool.

Add powdered sugar and vanilla to cooled mixture; beat until smooth. Yield: enough for one cake roll.

TIPSY CAKE

5 eggs, separated
2 tablespoons water
1 teaspoon grated lemon rind
1 tablespoon lemon juice
1 cup sugar
½ teaspoon salt
1½ cups sifted all-purpose
   flour
1½ teaspoons baking
   powder
⅓ cup butter or margarine,
   melted
1 cup sherry
½ cup blanched almonds
1 cup apple jelly
Creamy Custard Filling
2 cups whipping cream,
   whipped

Place egg yolks in a large mixing bowl; beat 6 minutes at high speed of electric mixer or until thick and lemon colored. Combine water, lemon rind, and juice; add to egg yolks. Beat on low speed of electric mixer until thoroughly blended. Beat at medium speed an additional 4 minutes or until thick.

Gradually beat in sugar and salt; continue beating about 5 to 6 minutes until smooth.

Combine flour and baking powder. Sprinkle flour mixture over yolk mixture ¼ cup at a time; carefully fold in. Gently fold melted butter into batter.

Beat egg whites (at room temperature) until soft peaks form. Gently fold about 1 cup of egg whites into yolk mixture. Gently fold yolk mixture into remaining egg whites.

Pour batter into an ungreased 10-inch tube pan, spreading evenly with a spatula. Bake at 350° for 35 minutes or until cake springs back when lightly touched. Remove cake from oven, and invert pan. Cool cake 40 minutes, and remove cake from pan.

Slice cake horizontally, making 2 separate layers. Pour ½ cup sherry over bottom layer; press ¼ cup almonds into cake and spread ½ cup apple jelly over almonds. Cover with remaining layer, and repeat procedure with remaining sherry, almonds, and jelly.

Spread Creamy Custard Filling over entire cake; frost with whipped cream just before serving. Yield: one 10-inch cake.

Creamy Custard Filling:

1 tablespoon all-purpose
   flour
1 tablespoon cornstarch
⅓ cup sugar
¼ teaspoon salt
1 cup milk
1 egg yolk
¼ teaspoon vanilla extract
1 teaspoon butter or
   margarine

Combine flour, cornstarch, sugar, and salt in a heavy saucepan; gradually stir in milk. Cook over medium heat, stirring constantly, until thick and bubbly.

Beat egg yolk until thick and lemon colored. Gradually stir in one-fourth of the hot mixture into yolk; add to remaining hot mixture, stirring constantly.

Cook over medium heat, stirring constantly, about 2 minutes or until thickened. Stir in vanilla and butter; cool. Chill 30 minutes. Yield: about 1 cup.

ORANGE JELLYROLL

3 eggs, separated
1¼ cups sugar, divided
1 teaspoon grated orange rind
½ cup fresh orange juice
1½ cups sifted cake flour
1½ teaspoons baking powder
¼ teaspoon salt
About 3 to 4 tablespoons
  sifted powdered sugar
1 cup grape or blackberry
  preserves
Additional sifted powdered
  sugar

Grease a 15- x 10- x 1-inch jel-lyroll pan with vegetable oil, and line with waxed paper. Grease waxed paper with vegetable oil; set aside.

Beat egg yolks until thick and lemon colored; gradually add 1 cup sugar, beating constantly. Set aside.

Combine orange rind and juice in a small saucepan; bring to a boil. Remove from heat, and stir into yolk mixture. Beat egg whites until foamy; gradually add remaining ¼ cup sugar, beating until stiff but not dry. Fold yolk mixture into egg whites. Combine flour, baking powder, and salt; fold into egg mixture. Spread batter into pre-pared pan. Bake at 350° for 15 minutes.

Sift 3 to 4 tablespoons pow-dered sugar in a 15- x 10-inch rectangle on a linen towel. When cake is done, immediately loosen from sides of pan and turn out onto sugar. Peel off waxed paper. Starting at narrow end, roll up cake and towel to-gether; cool on a wire rack, seam side down.

Unroll cake and remove towel; spread with preserves and reroll. Place on serving plate, seam side down; sprinkle with additional sifted powdered sugar. Chill until serving time. Yield: 8 to 10 servings.

TENDER LEMON SPONGE ROLL

5 eggs, separated
1 cup sugar
½ cup water
1 teaspoon grated lemon rind
1 tablespoon lemon juice
1 cup all-purpose flour
About 3 to 4 tablespoons
  sifted powdered sugar
Orange Filling
Additional sifted powdered
  sugar

Grease a 15- x 10- x 1-inch jel-lyroll pan with vegetable oil, and line with waxed paper. Grease waxed paper with vegetable oil; set aside.

Beat egg yolks in a large mix-ing bowl until thick and lemon colored; set aside.

Combine sugar and water in a medium saucepan; cook over medium heat, stirring con-stantly, until mixture reaches thread stage (234°). Remove from heat; slowly pour syrup into egg yolks, beating con-stantly, about 5 minutes or until mixture is cool. Stir in lemon rind and juice.

Beat egg whites (at room tem-perature) until stiff peaks form. Gently fold about half of the whites into yolk mixture. Sprin-kle flour over batter; fold in gently. Fold remaining whites into batter. Spread batter evenly in prepared pan. Bake at 350° for 15 minutes.

Sift 3 to 4 tablespoons pow-dered sugar in a 15- x 10-inch rectangle on a linen towel. When cake is done, immediately loosen from sides of pan, and turn out onto sugar. Peel off waxed paper. Starting at narrow end, roll up cake and towel to-gether; cool on a wire rack, seam side down.

Unroll cake and remove towel; spread with Orange Filling and reroll. Place on serving plate, seam side down; sprinkle with additional sifted powdered sugar. Chill until serving time. Yield: 8 to 10 servings.

*Second division cookery
class of a Washington, D.C.
high school, 1899*

Orange Filling:

3 eggs, beaten
¼ cup plus 2 tablespoons
  sugar
3 tablespoons butter or
  margarine
1 tablespoon plus 1½
  teaspoons grated orange
  rind
¾ cup orange juice
1 tablespoon plus 1½
  teaspoons lemon juice

Combine all ingredients in top of double boiler, and bring water to a boil. Reduce heat to low; cook, stirring constantly, until thickened. Chill. Yield: about 1 cup.

LEMON ROLL

5 eggs, separated
1 cup sugar
1 tablespoon grated lemon
  rind
2 tablespoons lemon
  juice
1 cup sifted cake flour
¼ teaspoon salt
About 3 to 4 tablespoons
  sifted powdered sugar
Tart Lemon Filling
Additional sifted powdered
  sugar

Grease a 15- x 10- x 1-inch jel-lyroll pan with vegetable oil, and line with waxed paper. Grease waxed paper with vegetable oil; set aside.

Beat egg yolks until thick and lemon colored; gradually add sugar, beating constantly. Stir in lemon rind and juice.

Beat egg whites, (at room temperature) until stiff peaks form. Fold yolk mixture into whites. Combine flour and salt; fold into egg mixture. Spread batter evenly in prepared pan. Bake at 350° for 15 minutes.

Sift 3 to 4 tablespoons powdered sugar in a 15- x 10-inch rectangle on a linen towel. When cake is done, immediately loosen from sides of pan, and turn out onto sugar. Peel off waxed paper. Starting at narrow end, roll up cake and towel together; cool on a wire rack, seam side down.

Unroll cake and remove towel. Spread with Tart Lemon Filling; reroll. Place on serving plate, seam side down; sprinkle with sifted powdered sugar. Chill at least 1 hour before serving. Yield: 8 to 10 servings.

Tart Lemon Filling:

1 cup sugar
3 tablespoons cornstarch
½ teaspoon salt
1 cup water
2 tablespoons butter or
  margarine
2 tablespoons grated lemon
  rind
½ cup lemon juice

Combine first 5 ingredients in a medium saucepan, stirring well; bring to a boil, and boil 1 minute. Reduce heat to low; cook, stirring constantly, until thickened. Remove from heat, and stir in rind and juice. Chill. Yield: about 1 cup.

FINISHING TOUCHES

T ime now to put the icing on the cake! That is, unless we are looking at a perfectly formed pound cake or angel food that can stand on its own merit, with perhaps a drift of powdered sugar sifted over the top to enhance its simplicity.

In choosing a frosting, think flavor combinations: peppermint on chocolate cake, or chocolate or coconut on vanilla butter cake; lemon on lemon, or orange on orange, for emphasis.

If the cake in question is for a special occasion, such as Valentine Day or Halloween or St. Patrick's Day, look to your vials of food colors. You may tint coconut green, if it is St. Pat's Day and you adore coconut: put a few drops of green food coloring into a plastic bag, rub the outside of the bag to make sure the inside of the bag is colored, add the coconut, and shake and knead it until the coconut takes the color.

A birthday for a special person? By all means the honoree should have his heart's desire, even if it is an Apple Cider Pound Cake with chocolate frosting, or a yellow butter cake with green icing. Who is to say he's wrong? Well, even the most indulgent cook might draw the line at a blue cake.

What is the time element? A real hurry-up cake will probably be served without frosting, or with a frosting baked on. But if it is to be frosted at all, it is worthwhile to select and prepare it carefully. Cooked frostings take more time than uncooked ones, and some require the use of a candy thermometer. The thermometer will pay for itself many times over; no more undercooked run-offs or overboiled mixtures that set up before they can be spread.

For the baker who wants his product to look as delectable as it tastes, close attention to the directions in this chapter will produce tempting results. If you simply want to write "Happy Birthday, Celeste," use the old paper cone trick, or poke a hole in the corner of a plastic bag, spoon in some icing, squeeze it down into the corner, and write away.

Cake decorating has grown in popularity of late years, thanks to the shops that have sprung up to sell decorating equipment. The classes they give are usually quite inexpensive because the shop wants to sell the tools of the trade. Take the lessons, by all means, but don't buy out the store. A basic cake decorating kit only costs a very few dollars.

From back to front: Quick Chocolate Frosting (page 137) swirls up the sides of the layer cake. Peppermint Frosting (page 133) is a variation of Divinity. Lemon Butter Cream Frosting (page 135) tops off a rolled cake.

COOKED FROSTINGS

CARAMELIZED FROSTING

3 cups sugar
1 cup butter
1½ cups warm milk (105° to 115°)

Combine sugar and butter in a 10-inch cast-iron skillet; cook over medium heat, stirring constantly, until sugar dissolves and becomes a golden syrup.

Gradually add warm milk to syrup mixture in skillet, stirring constantly. Continue to cook over medium heat, stirring constantly, until mixture reaches soft ball stage (240°).

Remove from heat; beat at medium speed of electric mixer about 3 to 5 minutes or until thick enough to spread. Spread immediately on cooled cake. Yield: enough for one (8-inch) 3-layer cake.

Step 1—Combine sugar and butter in a 10-inch cast-iron skillet; cook over medium heat, stirring constantly, until sugar dissolves and becomes a golden syrup.

Step 4—Remove from heat, and beat at medium speed of electric mixer about 3 to 5 minutes or until thick enough to spread.

Step 5—Spread frosting immediately between layers of cake within 1 to 1½ inch of cake edge.

Step 2—Gradually add warm milk to syrup mixture in skillet, stirring constantly.

Step 3—Continue to cook over medium heat, stirring constantly, about 20 minutes, until mixture reaches soft ball stage (240°). Mixture will be bubbly and golden brown in color.

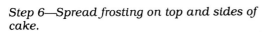

Step 6—Spread frosting on top and sides of cake.

Step 7—Allow frosting to set slightly before serving.

DIVINITY FROSTING

2½ cups sugar
⅛ teaspoon salt
½ cup light corn syrup
½ cup water
2 egg whites
1½ teaspoons vanilla extract
¾ cup chopped pecans

Combine sugar, salt, syrup, and water in a heavy saucepan. Cook over medium heat, stirring frequently, until mixture comes to a boil and sugar is dissolved. Continue cooking until the mixture reaches soft ball stage (240°).

Beat egg whites (at room temperature) until foamy. While beating at medium speed of electric mixer, slowly pour one-third of hot syrup in a thin stream over egg whites.

Cook remaining two-thirds of syrup to firm ball stage (248°). Slowly pour remaining syrup over egg white mixture while beating at medium speed of electric mixer. Turn mixer to high speed, and continue beating until stiff peaks form and frosting is thick enough to spread. Stir in vanilla and pecans. Spread immediately on cooled cake. Yield: enough for one (9-inch) 2-layer cake.

ORANGE FROSTING

2 cups sugar
1 cup water
2 egg whites
2 tablespoons grated orange rind
2½ tablespoons orange juice

Combine sugar and water in a medium-size heavy saucepan. Cook over medium heat, stirring frequently, until mixture comes to a boil and sugar is dissolved. Continue cooking, stirring frequently, until mixture reaches soft ball stage (240°).

Beat egg whites (at room temperature) until foamy. While beating at medium speed of electric mixer, slowly pour half of the hot syrup in a thin stream over egg whites. Return remaining syrup to heat, and continue cooking until mixture reaches hard ball stage (260°).

Continue beating at medium speed of electric mixer, and slowly pour remaining syrup in a thin stream over egg white mixture. Turn mixer to high speed, and beat until thick enough to spread. Add orange rind and juice; beat until blended. Spread immediately on cooled cake. Yield: enough for one (9-inch) 2-layer cake.

Advertisement for Florida oranges

LEMON SEVEN-MINUTE FROSTING

1½ cups sugar
2 egg whites
1 tablespoon light corn syrup
3 tablespoons water
2 tablespoons lemon juice
1 tablespoon lemon rind

Combine sugar, egg whites (at room temperature), and syrup in top of a large double boiler. Add water and lemon juice, and beat on low speed of an electric mixer for 30 seconds or just until blended.

Place over boiling water; beat constantly on high speed of electric mixer about 7 minutes or until stiff peaks form. Remove from heat. Add lemon rind; beat until frosting is thick enough to spread. Spread on cooled cake. Yield: enough for one (9-inch) 2-layer cake.

SEA FOAM FROSTING

1½ cups firmly packed brown sugar
2 egg whites
⅓ cup water
⅛ teaspoon salt
1 teaspoon almond extract

Combine sugar, egg whites (at room temperature), water, and salt in top of double boiler; place over boiling water, and stir constantly until sugar dissolves. Beat on high speed of electric mixer for 7 minutes or until frosting is fluffy and holds soft peaks. Remove from heat; stir in flavoring. Yield: enough for one (8-inch) 3-layer cake.

PEPPERMINT SILHOUETTE FROSTING

1½ cups sugar
1 tablespoon light corn syrup
¾ cup water
2 egg whites
2 to 3 drops peppermint oil
2 (1-ounce) squares unsweetened chocolate, melted

Combine sugar, syrup, and water in a medium-size heavy saucepan. Cook over medium heat, stirring frequently, until mixture comes to a boil and sugar is dissolved. Continue cooking, stirring frequently, until mixture reaches soft ball stage (240°).

Beat egg whites (at room temperature) until foamy. While beating at medium speed of electric mixer, slowly pour half of the hot syrup in a thin stream over whites. Return remaining syrup to heat, and continue cooking until mixture reaches hard ball stage (260°).

Continue beating at medium speed of electric mixer, and slowly pour remaining syrup in a thin stream over egg whites. Turn mixer to high speed, and continue beating until stiff peaks form and frosting is thick enough to spread. Add peppermint oil; beat until blended. Spread immediately on cooled cake. Drizzle melted chocolate over frosting. Yield: enough for one 10-inch tube cake.

The Seven-Minute Frosting group, such as Lemon, Sea Foam, and Peppermint, will yield attractive results when made by the clock. For other cooked frostings, a candy thermometer will help to achieve perfection by taking the guesswork out. This group includes Caramelized Frosting and Divinity.

PEPPERMINT FROSTING

1½ cups sugar
2 egg whites
1 tablespoon light corn syrup
¼ cup plus 1 tablespoon water
½ cup finely crushed peppermint candy

Combine sugar, egg whites, and syrup in top of a large double boiler; add water, and beat on low speed of electric mixer for 30 seconds or just until blended.

Place over boiling water; beat constantly on high speed of electric mixer about 7 minutes or until stiff peaks form. Remove from heat.

Add crushed peppermint, and beat 2 additional minutes or until frosting is thick enough to spread. Spread frosting on cooled cake. Yield: enough for one (8-inch) 3-layer cake.

Note: Additional crushed peppermint may be used to garnish frosting.

Who can resist a taste when the frosting is peppermint?

BLUEGRASS WHITE BOURBON FROSTING

1½ cups sugar
⅓ cup plus 1 teaspoon water
⅛ teaspoon salt
1 tablespoon bourbon
  whiskey
1 teaspoon lemon extract
2 egg whites
¼ teaspoon cream of tartar

Combine sugar, water, and salt in a medium-size heavy saucepan. Cook over medium heat, stirring frequently, until mixture comes to a boil and sugar is dissolved. Continue cooking, stirring frequently, until mixture reaches soft ball stage (240°). Stir in bourbon and flavoring.

Beat egg whites (at room temperature) until foamy; add cream of tartar. Beat at medium speed of electric mixer, slowly pouring hot syrup in a thin stream over egg whites. Turn mixer to high speed, and continue beating until stiff peaks form and frosting is thick. Spread immediately on cooled cake. Yield: enough for one (9-inch) 2-layer cake.

FLUFFY WHITE ICING

1½ cups light corn syrup
4 egg whites
½ cup sifted powdered
  sugar
1 teaspoon vanilla extract
2 cups grated coconut
  (optional)

Place syrup in a small saucepan; cook over medium heat, stirring frequently, until syrup reaches soft ball stage (240°).

Beat egg whites (at room temperature) until foamy. While beating at low speed of electric mixer, add sugar. Turn mixer to medium speed, and continue beating while slowly pouring hot syrup in a thin stream over egg whites. Continue beating until stiff peaks form and frosting is thick enough to spread. Add vanilla; beat until blended. Spread immediately on cooled cake. Sprinkle with grated coconut, if desired. Yield: enough for one (9-inch) 3-layer cake.

SEVEN-MINUTE WHITE FROSTING

1½ cups sugar
2 egg whites
1 tablespoon light corn
  syrup
¼ teaspoon cream of tartar
¼ cup plus 1 tablespoon
  cold water
1 teaspoon vanilla extract

Combine sugar, egg whites (at room temperature), syrup, and cream of tartar in top of a large double boiler; add water, and beat on low speed of electric mixer for 30 seconds or just until blended.

Place over rapidly boiling water; beat constantly on high speed of electric mixer about 7 minutes or until stiff peaks form. Remove from heat. Add vanilla; beat 2 to 3 minutes or until frosting is thick enough to spread. Spread on cooled cake. Yield: enough for one (8-inch) 3-layer cake.

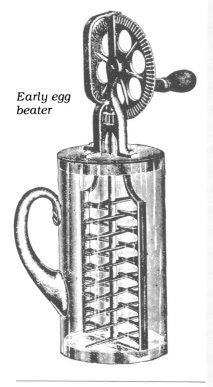

Early egg beater

QUICK FROSTINGS

BROWNED BUTTER FROSTING

⅔ cup butter
3 cups sifted powdered
    sugar
About 2 tablespoons hot
    water
1 teaspoon vanilla extract

Place butter in a heavy sauce-pan. Cook over low heat until golden brown, stirring frequently. Remove from heat; gradually add sugar, beating well. Add hot water as needed for spreading consistency. Stir in vanilla. Yield: enough for one (8-inch) 2-layer cake.

TANGY CITRUS ICING

2 tablespoons grated orange
    rind
About 2 tablespoons orange
    juice
About 2 tablespoons lemon
    juice
1 (16-ounce) package
    powdered sugar, sifted

Combine rind and juice in a large mixing bowl. Gradually stir in sugar. Beat on medium speed of electric mixer until mixture is smooth and creamy. Add additional juice to obtain spreading consistency, if necessary. Spread immediately on cooled cake. Yield: enough for one 10-inch tube cake.

Note: This icing has a strong citrus flavor, making it an ideal topping for Sweet Potato Pound Cake (page 56) or any other plain cake.

LEMON BUTTER CREAM FROSTING

⅔ cup butter or margarine,
    softened
3 cups sifted powdered
    sugar
1 teaspoon grated lemon
    rind
2 tablespoons lemon extract
6 drops yellow food coloring

From an early advertising brochure

Cream butter; gradually add sugar, beating well. Add remaining ingredients; beat until smooth. Yield: enough for one (9-inch) 3-layer cake.

Note: Additional lemon rind and lemon slices may be used as a garnish.

Children stirring chocolate frosting

SORGHUM CARAMEL FROSTING

¼ cup butter or margarine, melted
1 to 2 tablespoons sorghum molasses
2½ cups sifted powdered sugar
1 tablespoon milk
1 teaspoon vanilla extract

Combine butter and molasses, beating well. Gradually add sugar alternately with milk, mixing well after each addition. Add vanilla; beat until smooth. Yield: enough for one (8-inch) 2-layer cake.

PEANUT BUTTER SPICE FROSTING

½ cup plus 1 tablespoon creamy peanut butter
6 cups powdered sugar, sifted
1½ teaspoons ground cinnamon
1½ teaspoons ground nutmeg
¾ cup milk

Cream peanut butter. Combine sugar, cinnamon, and nutmeg; add to creamed peanut butter alternately with milk. Beat on medium speed of electric mixer until mixture is smooth. Yield: enough for one (8-inch) 3-layer cake.

STAY-SOFT FROSTING

3 egg whites
1½ cups sifted powdered sugar
½ teaspoon vanilla extract

Beat egg whites (at room temperature) until stiff peaks form. Gradually add sugar, beating well after each addition. Add vanilla; beat well. Spread on cooled cake. Yield: enough for one (8-inch) 3-layer cake.

Our so-called quick frostings depend upon powdered sugar for body. Please note that the word "sifted" appears before the sugar, and you'll never regret it. Frostings that are based on something hot, as in Browned Butter, are difficult to tell from the cooked frostings. Frostings made on a cold base, as in Lemon Butter, Rich Chocolate, and Peanut Butter Spice Frosting, it will be noted, are strongly flavored, which serves to obviate the sometimes "raw" taste of powdered sugar.

SEPTEMBER 1 2 3 4 5 6 7 8 9 10 11 12 13 14 15 16
17 18 19 20 21 22 23 24 25 26 27 28 29 30

HOUSEHOLD
SUGAR CARD   N⁰ 14451

Name *Jo. B. Palmer.*
Address *Platthill*
Number in Family *4*   Allowance per Month *18*
Amount on Hand *8*
I agree not to use sugar in excess of **TWO** lbs. per person a month
Signed *J. B. Palmer*
Issued by *A.V.P. Trustee*   Location *Water St.*
THIS CARD MUST BE TURNED IN TO OBTAIN A NEW ONE

OCT. 15 16
14
12 13
10 11
9
6 7
3
1 2

NOV. 1 2 3 4 5 6 7 8 9 10 11 12 13 14 15 16
17 18 19 20 21 22 23 24 25 26 27 28 29 30

Chocolate advertising photograph, 1880s

QUICK CHOCOLATE FROSTING

⅓ cup butter or margarine
½ cup evaporated milk
⅛ teaspoon salt
1 (6-ounce) package
   semisweet chocolate
   morsels
About 3 cups sifted powdered
   sugar

Combine butter, milk, and salt in a heavy saucepan; cook over medium heat, stirring constantly, until butter is melted. Remove from heat. Add chocolate morsels, and beat until smooth; cool.

Gradually add sugar, beating until thick enough to spread. If necessary, add additional sugar to obtain spreading consistency. Yield: enough for one (8-inch) 2-layer cake.

GLOSSY CHOCOLATE FROSTING

3 (1-ounce) squares
   semisweet chocolate
¼ cup butter or margarine
1½ cups sifted powdered
   sugar
3 tablespoons boiling water
1 teaspoon vanilla extract
¼ teaspoon almond extract

Melt chocolate and butter in top of a double boiler over hot water. Remove from heat, and add sugar; beat well. Add water and flavorings; beat until smooth (mixture will be slightly thin). Yield: enough for one (10-inch) tube cake.

CHOCOLATE FROSTING

¼ cup butter or margarine,
   softened
1 (16-ounce) package
   powdered sugar, sifted
3 tablespoons milk
1 (1-ounce) square
   unsweetened chocolate,
   melted

Cream butter in a large mixing bowl; gradually add sugar alternately with milk, beating mixture well.

Add melted chocolate, and beat until frosting is well blended. Yield: enough for one (9-inch) 2-layer cake.

RICH CHOCOLATE FROSTING

½ cup butter or margarine,
   softened
3½ cups sifted powdered
   sugar
2 tablespoons cocoa
2 tablespoons strong
   coffee
1 teaspoon vanilla
   extract

Cream butter. Combine sugar and cocoa; gradually add to butter alternately with coffee, beating well. Add vanilla; beat until mixture is smooth. Yield: enough for one (9-inch) 2-layer cake.

RECIPE CREDITS

Ambrosia Cake, Chocolate Ribbon Cake, Ice Cream Cake, Orange Jellyroll, Peanut Butter Spice Frosting, Peppermint Frosting, Prunella Cake, Thanksgiving Mincemeat Cake, Toasted Coconut Cake, White and Yellow Cake adapted from *Favorite Dallas County Recipes*, compiled by The Dallas County Home Demonstration Clubs, Dallas, Texas. By permission of Dallas County Agriculture Extension Service, Dallas.

Ambrosia Cake Filling, Delicate Cupcakes, Devil's Food Cake, Nobby Apple Cake, Wacky Cake adapted from *Recipes from Old Virginia*, compiled by The Virginia Federation of Home Demonstration Clubs, © 1946. By permission of the Virginia Extension Homemakers Council.

Apple Cider Pound Cake, Easter Orange Coconut Cake, Praline Chiffon Cake adapted from *State Fair of Texas Prize Winning Recipes*, edited and compiled by Elizabeth Peabody, Creative Arts Director, State Fair of Texas, Dallas, Texas. By permission of Elizabeth Peabody, State Fair of Texas.

Auntie's Apple Cake, Cottonwood Carrot Cake, South Carolina Fresh Peach Cake adapted from *Caterin' To Charleston* by Gloria Mann Maynard, Meredith Maynard Chase, Holly Maynard Jenkins. By permission of Merritt Publishing Co., Charleston, South Carolina, © 1981.

Blue Ribbon White Cake from the files of Mrs. Edward Sweeney, San Antonio, Texas, courtesy of Mrs. George Ames, adapted from *Flavors* by the Junior League of San Antonio, Texas, © 1978. By permission of the Junior League of San Antonio.

Bringhurst Pecan Cake, City Hall Coffee Cake, Old-Fashioned Chewy Fudge Cake adapted from *Harris County Heritage Society Cook Book*, published by the Harris County Heritage Society, Houston, Texas, © 1964. By permission of the Harris County Heritage Society.

Browned Butter Frosting, Mount Vernon Cake, Stay-Soft Frosting adapted from *Dear Daughter* by Ella Mae Tucker, Marionville, Missouri. By permission of Ella Mae Tucker.

Cake Fingers, Chocolate Groom's Cake, Chocolate Pound Cake, Gretchen's Cracker Cake, Hot Water Chocolate Cake, Red Watermelon Cake adapted from *The Texas Cookbook* by Mary Faulk Koock and Rosalind Cole, Austin, Texas, © 1965. By permission of Mary Faulk Koock.

Cherry Upside-Down Cake courtesy of Mrs. Ruth Drum, Rowlett, Texas.

Chocolate Chiffon adapted from *Memorial Book and Recipes—1957*, compiled by Mrs. Marie Baca for the Czech Catholic Home for the Aged, Inc., Hillje, Texas. By permission of The Board of Trustees, Czech Catholic Home for the Aged, Inc.

Chocolate "Failure" Cake adapted from *Recipes of Pioneer Women & Their Relations*, complied by The Cass County Genealogical Society, Atlanta, Texas, © 1974. By permission of The Cass County Genealogical Society.

Chocolate Midgets adapted from *Buckner Heritage Cookbook 1879-1979*, edited and compiled by Buckner Heritage Cookbook Committee, Dallas, Texas. By permission of Buckner Baptist Benevolences, © 1978.

Chocolate Sheath Cake courtesy of Mrs. Clint Wyrick, Garland, Texas.

Coffee Angel Food Cake adapted from *The Helen Corbitt Collection*, edited by Elizabeth Ann Johnson, copyright © 1981. By permission of Houghton Mifflin Co.

Confederate Soldiers, Grandma's Chew Bread adapted from The *Texas Press Women's Cookbook*, compiled by Donna Hunt, Kathy Pill, Bobbi Field for Texas Press Women, Inc., Austin, Texas. By permission of Lone Star Publishers, Inc., © 1976.

Delicious Banana Layer Cake courtesy of Mrs. Vernice Maples, Dallas, Texas.

Dried Apple Cake courtesy of Mrs. T. Ray Morgan, Birmingham, Alabama.

Fig Preserves Cake, Traditional Wedding Fruitcake adapted from *The Mississippi Cookbook*, compiled and edited by the Home Economics Division of the Mississippi Cooperative Extension Service. By permission of University Press of Mississippi, Hattiesburg, Mississippi, © 1972.

Halloween Date Fudge Cake adapted from *The Wide, Wide World of Texas Cooking* by Morton Gill Clark, © 1970. By permission of Harper & Row Publishers, Inc., New York.

Heritage Jam Cake courtesy of Mrs. Charles De Haven, Owensboro, Kentucky.

Hootenholler Whiskey Cake courtesy of Mrs. Joseph H. Santen, Mooresburg, Tennessee.

Jennie Benedict's Rum Cake adapted from *The Southern Cook Book* by Marion Brown. By permission of the University of North Carolina Press, Chapel Hill, North Carolina, © 1951.

Jiffy Chocolate Cake, Texas Brandy Pound Cake, Whipped Cream Cake adapted from *Favorite Recipes of Texas*. By permission of Favorite Recipes Press, Nashville, Tennessee. © 1965.

La Reine Cake (The Queen) adapted from *Talk About Good!* by the Junior League of Lafayette Publications, Lafayette, Louisiana. © 1967. By permission of The Junior League of Lafayette.

"Little Nanny's" Blackberry Jam Cake courtesy of Mrs. Ann L. Richardson, Birmingham, Alabama.

Mahogany Cake adapted from *Southern Cooking* by Mrs. S.R. Dull. © 1941. By permission of Grosset & Dunlap, New York.

Marble Molasses Cake, Praline Cake adapted from *River Road Recipes* by The Junior League of Baton Rouge, Inc., Baton Rouge, Louisiana. © 1959. By permission of The Junior League of Baton Rouge, Inc.

Minnehaha Cake adapted from *Southern Sideboards* by the Junior League of Jackson, Mississippi. © 1978. By permission of the Junior League of Jackson.

Mocha Pound Cake courtesy of Mrs. M.A. Jordan, Katemcy, Texas.

Old-Fashioned Strawberry Shortcake courtesy of Mrs. Geneva P. Tobias, Albemarle, North Carolina.

Peanut-Apple Squares, Welcome Cake adapted from *Tullie's Receipts*, compiled by the Kitchen Guild of the Tullie Smith House Restoration, Atlanta Historical Society, Atlanta, Georgia. © 1976. By permission of the Atlanta Historical Society.

Pecan-Topped Chocolate Pound Cake, White Fruitcake courtesy of Verda McCullough, Jayees, Mississippi.

Pineapple Meringue Cake courtesy of the family of Jerry Skipwith, Grand Saline, Texas.

Sam Houston White Cake adapted from *125th Anniversary Cookbook* by Imperial Sugar Co., Sugarland, Texas. © 1968. By permission of Tracy-Locke/BBDO, Dallas, Texas.

Sauerkraut Cake adapted from *Through Our Kitchen Door* by The Guild, Dallas County Heritage Society, Inc., Dallas, Texas. © 1978. By permission of The Dallas County Heritage Society.

Scotch Spice Cake courtesy of Mrs. Henry W. Keyser, Jr., Mason, Texas.

Self-Frosting Angel Cake courtesy of Mrs. A.R. Davis, Jr., Garland, Texas.

Shenandoah Dark Fruitcake courtesy of Mrs. Juanita Caskey, Lancaster, Virginia.

Short'nin' Bread courtesy of Mrs. Wanda A. Beasley, Columbia, Mississippi.

Snowball Cake adapted from the *Atlanta Woman's Club Cookbook*, compiled and edited by the Atlanta Woman's Club, Atlanta, Georgia. By permission of the Atlanta Woman's Club.

Stellar's Funeral Cakes courtesy of Cynthia Smith, Liberty, Texas.

Tennessee Stack Cake courtesy of Dorothy Beeler, Nashville, Tennessee.

Tennessee Upside-Down Apple Cake adapted from *Mountain Makin's in the Smokies* by the Great Smoky Mountains Natural History Association, Gatlinburg, Tennessee. © 1957. By permission of the Great Smoky Mountains Natural History Association.

White Wonder Cake adapted from *The Woman's Club of Fort Worth Cook Book*, compiled and edited by Mrs. W. Wayne Wallace and Mrs. Joe. R. Wallis. By permission of the Woman's Club of Fort Worth, Fort Worth, Texas, © 1955.

Williamsburg Pork Cake adapted from the original antique recipe for Pork Cake in *The Williamsburg Art of Cookery* by Helen Bullock. By permission of Colonial Williamsburg Foundation, Williamsburg, Virginia. © 1938.

INDEX